WOMEN
AND
RELIGIOUS
RITUAL

WOMEN
AND
RELIGIOUS
RITUAL

Lesley A. Northup, Editor

The Pastoral Press
Washington, DC

ISBN: 1-56929-008-3

© The Pastoral Press, 1993

The Pastoral Press
225 Sheridan Street, N.W.
Washington, D.C. 20011
(202) 723-1254

The Pastoral Press is the Publications Division of the National Association of Pastoral Musicians, a membership organization of musicians and clergy dedicated to fostering the art of musical liturgy.

Printed in the United States of America

Contents

Preface

MUCH HAS BEEN WRITTEN OF LATE ABOUT WOMEN AND RELIGION—A
subject that, after a history of scholarly disinterest, is fast becoming a staple of university and seminary curricula. Like
other inquiries into women's lives, culture, and contributions,
it has benefitted from the research of diverse contemporary in-
vestigators—women's studies pioneers, feminist theologians,
biblical scholars, anthropologists, historians, psychologists,
and others. Their cumulative insights have demonstrated a
clear correlation between gender and religious behavior and
belief. At the same time, a movement toward the development
of a specifically feminist spirituality, rooted in historical scholarship but more deliberately dependent on experience, has increasingly appealed to women of all sorts and conditions.

At the intersection of these concerns is a largely unexplored
prior issue—ritual practice. If, as many scholars believe, ritual
precedes belief, faith, and even myth, this neglected category
is critical to a full understanding of women's religious life.
The articles in this book, therefore, consider how religious ritual affects and is affected by women. They thus attempt to
contribute to a broad-based foundation that can underlie and
support current investigations into such areas as feminist analysis, ritual criticism, and liturgical theology. In doing so, they
address a number of fundamental questions:

* Does ritual behavior differ with gender, and if so,
how?
* How have women's ritual roles been conditioned historically?

* Which rituals or ritualizations illuminate women's distinctive ritual needs?
* How does women's ritual participation vary in different cultural settings?
* What can attentive observation of women's ritual behavior tell us about relationships, institutions, and power?
* What unique contributions have women made to ritual development?
* What principles should guide the design of women's rituals?

To respond to these queries, this volume consciously incorporates the work of women from a variety of backgrounds, both cultural and scholarly. Authors include academicians, clinicians, and clergy. They discuss Judaism, Christianity, Islam, Woman-Church, and American cultural religion. They are Reform Jews, Evangelicals, Roman Catholics, Seventh-Day Adventists, agnostics, mainline Christians, New Agers, Anglicans. More importantly—and essential to any balanced investigation—they represent a broad range of fields: anthropology, folklore, psychology, liturgics, music, theology, pastoral care, ritual studies, history, women's studies, linguistics. That is, they mirror the vast network of contributors to the comprehensive study of religion. The result is a thoroughly interdisciplinary study that sheds new light on vital religious issues and on what it means to be a religious woman.

Keynoted by Sandy Sasso's moving tribute to a groundbreaking woman, the volume includes powerful statements of the interdependence of culture, religion, and gender. Melva Costen and Amitiyah Elayne Hyman write of the past and future of African American women of faith; Dana Everts-Boehm and Sheila Webster Boneham delve deep into the relationship of women and the supernatural in Latin American and Muslim cultures; Karen Sue Hybertsen traces the crossover of religious into domestic ritual in her discussion of Victorian Halloween observances. And Kathryn Allen Rabuzzi ventures beyond the boundaries of standard definitions in her reflections on gender masquerade as religious ritual in American culture.

The institutional traditions are examined and critiqued by Barbara Borts, who penetrates Jewish gender-defined space; Carole Rayburn, whose insights as a clinical psychologist inform her experience as a Seventh-Day Adventist; Anne Andersson, who examines the development of Latin American basic ecclesial communities in the light of feminist theology; and Linda Coleman, who documents one attempt of evangelical feminists to come to terms with dual allegiances. Shermie Shafer and Diann Neu discuss the evolution of new rituals for women, both in tandem with and apart from established forms of worship.

This collection presents not only a snapshot of how women worship and ritualize, but also performs a hermeneutical function, variously uncovering the *meaning* unfolding in those acts. It is only from such a perspective that women's experience of religious ritual can be fully understood. It is only with such an understanding that religious ritual—and, consequently, belief and praxis—can be fully critiqued and, where necessary, revised to meet the spiritual needs of women.

Introduction
"Unwrapping the Gift"

Sandy Eisenberg Sasso

OVER TWO THOUSAND YEARS AGO, SEVENTY MEN CLOISTERED IN SEP-
arate rooms, tradition tells us, wrote the Greek Septuagint, the
first translation of the Bible. On 21 March 1992 seventy women
joined to speak out together, to honor, and to celebrate with Judith Kaplan Eisenstein, the first Bat Mitzvah. Over two thousand years ago, seventy men wrote a translation out of their experience, a translation which influenced generations of those
who read the Bible. We must dare imagine what the gathering
of seventy women who seek to translate our sacred narratives
out of their experience will mean for generations yet to come.

Seventy years ago, Judith Kaplan, a young girl of twelve
and a half, stood in front of her congregation, as no woman
had done before, to recite the Torah blessings and read Torah
as a Bat Mitzvah. There was no fanfare, no front-page articles—"no thunder sounded, no lightning struck." It's a wonder how all great revolutions begin with what at first sight
seems only natural—like a black woman taking a seat at the
front of a bus, like a Jewish woman, really still a child, standing in front of a congregation reading Torah. On second sight,
it is an act of courage which becomes a gift unwrapped by future generations. What began that day with the determination
of a young girl and the wisdom of her father, Rabbi Mordecai
Kaplan, became a revolution in religious creativity. We are
still unwrapping that gift.

From birth to death, the ritual life of the religious community has been renewed. From welcoming girls into the covenant, from menarche to menopause, through infertility and miscarriage, through marriage and divorce, new landscapes are being sculpted from the soil of tradition.

Mordecai Kaplan, a leading twentieth-century American Jewish philosopher, called upon his generation to "free religious ritual from its bondage and legalism."[1] He recognized the need to fearlessly evaluate traditional symbols, not "merely to conserve or reform" but to "construct or reconstruct." He sought both to preserve revered custom and tradition and at the same time to revitalize old forms and give affirmation to new spiritual yearnings. For Kaplan, "folkways" are the social practices by which a people externalize the reality of their collective being. The more alive a people, the more they abound in affirmative folkways.[2] Kaplan understood that we cannot simply remake the past in the image of our beliefs, but we can discover customs and voices, write new stories, and make them a part of our sacred doing and remembering. As he taught a new generation of Jews, "When we . . . find ourselves without corroboration, or precedent in tradition for what we regard as true or just, we must seek to give effect to it . . . to refuse to do so would be to turn our back on truth and justice."[3]

The need for historic continuity and contemporary transformation of ritual is highlighted in Robert Bellah's distinction between tradition and traditionalism. For Bellah, traditionalism is marked by authoritarian closure whereas tradition allows for "reappropriation of the past in light of the present."[4] In the last few decades women have reappropriated the past in light of the present and have evolved and reinvigorated rituals and traditions which have enriched the spiritual life of the Jewish people. As one young mother commented to me after a ceremony for her new baby daughter, "Thank you for letting me speak. At the naming of my last child, I was silent. Now I feel included."

Rather than representing a break with tradition, new ritual and liturgical activity are the very essence of a living tradition. The authority to change or to reconstruct the prayer and ritual life of the community comes from tradition itself. It is the constant renewal of religious forms which keeps tradition vital and capable of giving meaning to each new generation of seekers.

Kaplan believed that "it is with ritual, not ideas, that religion begins."[5] And so it was with a ritual, a Bat Mitzvah, that the religious life of this century was renewed.

It is not easy to create or even reconstruct ritual. It is more than the weaving together of a few prayerful or poetic lines and symbolic acts. Rituals that last tug at the private heart and the communal soul. They resonate not only with the personal but with the transcendent. They help us make meaning of our private lives because they reach back to grasp that which is timeless, renewing tradition and traditionalizing the new. But Kaplan's challenge was to "look upon ourselves not merely as descendants but as ancestors of posterity, responsible for preserving and creating symbols and rituals for future generations."[6]

When my husband, Dennis, and I held open our daughter's tallit for her to recite the appropriate blessing for the first time as she became a Bat Mitzvah (May 1992), we knew that what she did was neither ancient nor hallowed by generations of women who did the same. Her grandmothers and great-grandmothers did not wrap themselves in fringed garments. When I first put on a tallit as an adult, I did so as much as an act of defiance as of affirmation. For my daughter, it was different; that tallit belonged to her, it was her right and responsibility to wrap herself within it as much as any boy's. And yet, this was not all that I knew or felt. As I placed the tallit around my daughter's shoulders, I felt the flow of the generations reaching back to the beginning of our history as a people. And God's words to Abraham became my words—"Go forth and be a blessing." And God's words to Debora are heard anew, spoken from mother to daughter. "Awake, awake, Debora, and sing your song."

Our daughter was privileged to have as guests on the Shabbat of her Bat Mitzvah Dr. Ira and Judith Kaplan Eisenstein. When Judith spoke to Debora, she said, "Right now I am the oldest and you are the youngest Bat Mitzvah." A single moment held seventy years of history, as a gracious and wise woman blessed a bright-eyed and promising daughter of Israel. At this one time filled with so many memories and so much hope, I heard ancestors' stories and grandparents' voices. All this embraced my daughter in an act that was both old and new.

Human stories are the narrative of life's cycle; ritual is the poetry that turns a personal transition into a holy pilgrimage. Our spiritual landscape has been filled with secret gardens, silences, and unrecorded journeys. With the first Bat Mitzvah began the speaking out of silence.   While both men and women have engaged in this ritual process, it has been the unwritten narratives of women's lives, newly spoken, that have shaped the contours of our religious renewal. Women's questions have helped us to sanctify those unmarked passages of time, the spaces left empty by the generations.

In a religious culture that dictates ritual from awakening until preparing for sleep, can there be the symbolic acts and holy words that sanctify the moment of learning of a pregnancy? In a faith which celebrates escape from danger with a prayer, can there be a prayer for the healing of a battered woman or an abused child? In a tradition that counts hundreds of blessings, can there be one blessing upon the birth of a daughter? In a community that counsels an intricate and comforting ritual of mourning, can there be a ceremony to carry a family through the sorrow of a miscarriage or stillbirth?

Women have taught us that religious revelation comes not only vertically, from on high, but horizontally, from within. We have always looked for spiritual truths atop some mountain, but we also have discovered that we can find religious truths and God in the human encounter, in our places of gathering. In this spirit and in honor of Judith Kaplan Eisenstein, beloved teacher and friend, I offer a new pilgrimage prayer.

> Must we always go up to some mountain
> with Abraham, with Isaac to Moriah?
> The air is so thin up there,
> and it's hard to breathe.
>
> Must we always go up to some mountain
> with Moses to Sinai?
> It's so far from the earth,
> and what's below appears so small
> You can forget it's real.
>
> Must we always go up to some mountain
> with Moses to Nebo?
> Climbing—there's only one way
> and loneliness.

Must we always go up to some mountain
with Elijah to Carmel?
The ascent is not hard.
It's the descending—
too easy to slip
with no one to catch your fall.

I'm weary of mountains
where we're always looking up
or looking down and sacrificing
so our neck hurts
and we need glasses.

Our feet upon the mountains
are blistered,
and our shoes are always wrong—
not enough "sole."

Can we sit with Sarah in a tent,
next to Deborah under a palm tree,
alongside Rebekkah by the well—
with Judith in the synagogue reading Torah,
to wash our feet,
to catch our breath
and our soul?

The religious imagination of the twentieth century has allowed us to catch our breath and our soul. Ritual is not simply handed down; it is shaped within community. It is not just acted out upon us, but we are the active participants in its drama. Barbara Myerhoff underscored the importance of our active relation to rituals as "constructed performances." "Instead of having rites performed on us, we do them to and for ourselves and immediately we are involved in a form of self-creation that is potentially community building . . ."[7] Our generation has not only created new ritual; it has transformed the ways in which we enact it, and in turn build community.

In the past decades, as legitimacy was given to ritual innovation within the religious community, all sorts of creations rushed in. We know that those creations are not final, but part of an ongoing process of humanity's sacred searching.

We have something to learn from the first Bat Mitzvah. It was a revolutionary, yet gentle step. Judith did not read directly from the Torah; she did not stand on the bimah. The message was conveyed in a definitive yet not shocking fashion, in a courageous but not jarring way. This enabled the ritual to make its entry into community and to grow into posterity, to become a sacred expectation, a stage in the Jewish life cycle.

What will remain and what will fade of ritual innovation will be determined by time and the community that celebrates and commemorates life's passages and the marking of time and seasons. Bat Mitzvah in one form or another is a permanent feature of almost every synagogue.[8] A welcoming ceremony for girls is an expectation of almost all new parents. The revival and reconstruction of Tu B'Shevat Sedarim[9] and Rosh Hodesh ceremonies are old forms invested with new meanings. New voices have been added to Jewish liturgy and holy day celebrations.

The story is told that when Picasso presented his portrait of Gertrude Stein, a critical viewer commented: "But it doesn't look like Gertrude Stein." To which Picasso responded, "It will." We may say the same of new ritual. To the comment that it doesn't look like tradition, we may respond, "It will."

We are still on the journey. There is a continuing need for ritual transformation which is both evocative of the past and resonant with the present. There are dangers on both sides of the ritual spectrum. On the one end, there is the innovator who affirms that every breath can be ritualized and on the other end is the traditionalist who believes all authoritative ritual has already been created and cannot be altered. We must navigate a course between a spiritual privatism which asserts that the holy can be completely custom-made, and a religious fundamentalism which claims that custom was made once and for all. We are in need of ritual that both honors the individual and the communal, tradition and change, the repetitive certainty of established acts and words and the refreshing spontaneity of improvisation. We are in need of ritual that will give expression to our innermost longings and deepest fears and call us to transcend the personal. Ritual must be more than a sacred affirmation of who we are; it must also be a holy challenge to what and who we may become in solidarity with a community of holy travelers.

Ritual does not only sanctify our moments of passage, it also obligates our being. The power of the covenantal birth ritual is in its ability to call forth joy at new life, but also to evoke awe of the responsibility we have to raise the child to Torah, huppah and good deeds. The power of Bat Mitzvah is not simply the celebration of emerging adolescence and the beginning of a parental letting go, but the handing on of values, and of stories, tears and laughter from one generation to the next in the hope that the ancient chain will continue through this newly responsible child. Good ritual is not a massage to our vulnerable selves, not private therapy. Ritual works, when it does, because it connects us to something beyond ourselves and places us in a community and tradition to which we are accountable and for which we are responsible.

How easy it is after seventy years, after increased opportunities for women and a resurgence of ritual creativity, to forget how extraordinary and how difficult and how lonely it was to take those first steps. How important it is for us to remember, to retell those early stories and to honor the struggle, and not to take all that we have received for granted. In a time of increasing fundamentalism that seeks to co-opt religious language and constrict the spiritual landscape, we must say the following.

We create ceremonies, we tell stories, we make and enliven rituals in the tradition of Sarah and Abraham, who celebrated Isaac's weaning; in the tradition of our ancestors, who taught a new generation not to sit in darkness but to light Sabbath candles; in the tradition of the rabbis, who told the Hannukah story of the cruze of oil and began a new custom which lasted for generations.[10] In their name, in the name of all those who went before them, and in the name of all those generations yet to come, we light candles, we preserve and we create. We marvel at how much remains the same in our cycles of time, what ancient words still move us, how different we are, what silences must still be broken. What really matters is not just that we are descendants, but that we are ancestors who bequeath our spiritual quest to the next generation.

We accept this awe-filled responsibility with a deep sense of humility. After all, who are we, tied as we are to our own time and place, to fashion the sacred words and create the holy drama to carry us through the passages of our years? We accept this responsibility with a strong sense of duty. After all, who are we, bearers of the image of God, not to pour our souls into the crucible of time, to affix our name to the holy narrative of our people?

One Shabbat seventy years ago, a young girl read the sacred words of our tradition and became a Bat Mitzvah. There was no thunder and there was no lightning (or perhaps there was), just a sacred affirmation of her belonging to a holy people. Who could have known then what would come of this one seemingly simple symbolic act? Thank you, Judith, for your first step, and for the steady hand and wise heart that guide us still.

Notes

1. Mordecai Kaplan, *The Future of the American Jew* (New York: Reconstructionist Press, 1967) 210.

2. Mordecai Kaplan, *Judaism as a Civilization* (New York: Jewish Reconstructionist Foundation, 1957) 431-433.

3. Mordecai Kaplan, *Questions Jews Ask* (New York: Reconstructionist Press, 1956) 435-437.

4. Robert Bellah and others, *Habits of the Heart* (Berkeley: University of California Press, 1985) 155.

5. Mordecai Kaplan, "Religion as the Symbolization of the Values of Holiness," in *Symbols and Values: An Initial Study*, ed. Lyman Bruser and Louis Finkelstein (New York, 1954) 189.

6. Kaplan, *The Future of the American Jew* 210.

7. Barbara Myerhoff, "Rites of Passage: Process and Paradox" in *Celebration Studies in Festivity and Ritual*, ed. Victor Turner (Washington, D.C.: Smithsonian Institution Press, 1982).

8. Bat Mitzvah has become an expectation of all Jewish girls between the ages of twelve and thirteen. Orthodox Judaism limits ritual participation and does not allow a woman to read Torah. Often the girls who do choose to become B'not Mitzvah in an Orthodox congregation offer a commentary on the meaning of the Shabbat Torah or Haftarah (prophetic) reading.

All Reconstructionist, Reform and most Conservative synagogues welcome the full and equal participation of girls as B'not Mitzvah. They chant Torah and Haftarah and lead in major parts of the liturgy. Whereas practice differs from congregation to congregation (some Conservative synagogues only permit girls to read the Haftarah or restrict their participation to Friday evening), most Jewish girls entering adolescence in the United States become B'not Mitzvah and many put on a tallit for the first time on this occasion.

9. A special meal modeled after a sixteenth-century Sephardic tradition which celebrates the Jewish new year of the trees and the renewal of nature.

10. The legend of the lights is not told in the Book of Maccabees which first chronicles the Hanukah events but appears centuries later in rabbinic literature as the basis for a new ritual.

WOMEN'S RITUAL TRADITION

1

African-American Women and Religious Ritual

Melva Wilson Costen

AFRICAN-AMERICAN WOMEN OF THE CHRISTIAN FAITH HAVE A LONG and continuous history of rituals which evolve from our African grounding in an insatiable hunger for God. This longing deepens when our status as an oppressed people is called to our attention and when societal patterns of behavior threaten to destroy us. Like Hagar, the African-American woman is constantly exploited and threatened with exile for responding as an obedient servant. Like Queen Vashti, she is courageous enough to refuse to compromise. Like Mary, the mother of Jesus, she can emerge from the margins of society to become blessed among women!

Rituals, in the broadest understanding, include all aspects and patterns of social behavior, spontaneous and structured, which help order and make sense out of life experiences. Through rituals and the ritualization process, persons and societies communicate their culture, values, symbols, and other language tools, as well as their understanding of the cosmos in relation to life. The repetitive nature of ritualized behavior serves a variety of functions. It helps in an analysis of contemporary situations and facilitates the application of meaning to life, while securing persons emotionally, spiritually and psychologically. Healthy rituals provide a ground of familiarity

3

and "sameness" that reassures continuity in human interaction and personal journeys that might be temporarily disordered. Rather than serving as an escape mechanism, rituals can allow a flexible balance between two extreme poles of human existence: complete disorder and confusion, and ordered direction.

For the first generation of Africans in America who understood and functioned with an awareness of the inseparableness of the "sacred and secular" aspects of life, all rituals were basically religious. The whole of life in Africa—from birth to death—involved some life-cycle ritual that shaped individuals and communities. Rituals to acknowledge, honor, and incorporate persons into the community before birth and after death helped expand an understanding of the importance of rituals. The concept of the extended community also considered plant and animal life, total creation, and the continuous creation process as part of the ritualization process. This heritage continued as people of African descent were socialized through a system of slavery and oppression as African-Americans.

The depth of this understanding has continued in the world-view of African-American women. In view of an historical "triple oppression" (race, sex, and class) we must begin with experiences in America as a point of departure for discussing African-American women and religious rituals. In this respect the concept of "womanist theology" is quite applicable. Created out of an awareness of the unique role of African-American women, the concept of "womanist" evolved from "womanish," a term created by African-American women to describe the "outrageous, audacious, and willful behavior" of female children who act grownup.[1] Womanist theologians have captured and built upon the essence of the meaning of this term in their shaping of Womanist theology. Jacqueline Grant is helpful in her observation that

> Womanist means being and acting out who you are and interpreting the reality for yourself.[2]

In retrospect, numerous "womanists" can be identified in the early history of the shaping of America in general and African-American liturgical theology and practices in particular. This began with the strong Black women (including but not limited to mothers) who participated in the struggle for the survival of African-American families and communities. In a continuation of the African world-view of non-compartmentalization of life, women played a dominant role in interpreting and responding to the existential milieu in which the community found itself. In a value-complex culture, women were in the forefront in reviewing and renewing the meaning of personal and community values in direct reference to the ever changing contexts of the marginalized slave community.

Basic to this was a survival ritualization process which carried over into ritual actions of worship. The ritualization process often began with the forced, premature motherhood of teenagers who had no control over demands made by male oppressors. The "normal" role of ritual in personal and social development by psychologists such as Erik Erikson and Erving Goffman did not apply to teenage mothers, suddenly thrust into a different level of awareness.[3]

It is no wonder that the concept of "womanist" emerged! Female children who were forced to assume the role of mother found it necessary to create a way to grow up suddenly and survive with some semblance of wholeness through intentionally shaped rituals. This might obviate some of the outrageous, audacious, courageous, and grownup "womanish" ritual behavior adopted even by non-teenage mothers. Adding to this dilemma was the problem of a general lack of psychological wholeness resulting from an oppressive system.

Religion and Religious Action

A pivotal point from which women could develop a secure inner core and stability, discern self, and establish directions was most often religion, more specifically, Christian religion. Building upon their African heritage, women in the slave society found solace in the meaning and message of the Christian faith. Promises of God in Jesus Christ became the foundation of hope, both in their personal and corporate lives. Christian faith and hope provided the impetus for drawing upon daily rituals for use in shaping religious rituals, both during and after slavery. Evidence abounds for the use of forms of rituals by women in the nurturing support of family—nuclear and extended. For this reason, religious rituals in this discussion will involve a dialectic between what is said and what is done in both the gathered and scattered worshiping community.

Worship in the Invisible Institution

The term, "invisible institution," coined in the twentieth century, is used to describe the variety of forms of church life and religious experiences of African-American slaves beyond the visible, authorized, institutional forms. Slaves who were introduced to Christianity during the seventeenth century, albeit reluctantly, were unable to participate holistically in the denominational liturgy of slaveholders as marginal members of churches of their oppressors. Since slaves were generally forbidden by slaveholders to gather privately without supervision for any reason—even to pray or worship—separate, secret, "invisible" places were created out of sight and sound of slaveholders. In secret places such as brush arbors ("hush harbors") and swamps, Christianity was of necessity indigenized, and new liturgical forms with new theological meanings were shaped and disseminated. Risking severe punishment, slave and free African-Americans created their own functional religious "institution" which was "invisible" to the Euro-Americans who, with mixed motives, had evangelized them.

While some slaves worshiped or participated as onlookers from segregated vantage points in Euro-American congregations, worship experiences were not limited to such places. In fact, slaves could not have considered such non-inclusive gatherings "liturgy" in the sense that ritual action was "the work of the people." True, authentic "liturgy" for the slaves could happen only in "invisible" institutions. Hidden from the oppressors, the particular worshiping community could shape and disseminate forms and styles reflective of a people called of God, but marginalized by a racist society.

According to numerous testimonies of ex-slaves, it is apparent that liturgical "calls to worship" would take place during regular times for work and even amid the insincere institutional worship organized and controlled by Euro-Americans. Thus, slaves of African descent could utilize the gifts of their African heritage to make the best of any situation. Symbolic actions and language usages imbedded in the world-view of African peoples were called upon as the foundation for liturgical action.

Songs and singing styles, influenced by their memories of fore-parents and of Africa, were combined with biblical texts and theological concepts to "announce" a time and place of meeting. Religious rituals before and during meetings focussed on freedom—freedom to worship God in Jesus the Christ and freedom from the bondage of slavery, if only for a moment!

A Different Understanding of Liturgy

Both women and men assumed leadership in the calling and conducting of religious meetings. The period of harsh slavery did not lend itself to a time of questioning sex-specific roles. There was no time to construct feminist or womanist liturgical traditions. This was a matter of life or death for a race of people who needed both males and females in order to survive. What is clear is that the liturgical life of this enslaved people was God's way of empowering a people to find meaning and remain whole persons in the midst of harsh struggles.

Slave women apparently understood that their experiences were somewhat different from those of the men in slavery. Nevertheless, they understood the necessity for their roles to be centered in whatever was best for the whole enslaved community. Without a "female-controlled" support group during the early shaping of liturgy, the focus was on ways that all slaves could worship as struggling people of God.

In their own way, women utilized their imaginative, artistic, creative, nurturing, and protective skills in the gathering, the gathered, and the scattered community. They were "liturgists," leading prayers and songs and reading Scriptures (if they were able). They were preachers, exhorters, storytellers, and teachers who challenged the community to keep the faith. They moved people through the kerygma of worship (ritual) to underground railroads to freedom (mission), and were often flogged or killed because of this. Women listened to God and then participated in the forging of ritual acts out of their commitment to group survival. They could not afford to be isolated in their concerns, for in many ways the slave community depended to a large extent on their female insight, instinct, and instruction. Religious rituals, founded upon faith in God who was "always on time," could not be confined to separate times for religious meetings.

Even without clear evidence, we can assume that women provided leadership in helping to make the invisible worshiping space as safe as possible from intruders. In order that African-American clandestine worshipers could feel free and safe in their "makeshift" liturgical environment, it was often necessary to improvise an acoustical space that could subdue the sound. This was done by encircling the open space with wet quilts suspended on bushes, fences, or cloth lines. Inverted washpots or washpots filled with water also helped to contain and subdue the sound. No doubt, these and other acoustical methods emanated from the ingenuity of some of the women.

Liturgical acts were filled with freedom and spontaneity, often attributed to women who were also listening above the enthusiasm, always in "creative" anticipation of a sudden need to cease activities and to flee the space. At all times during such secret worship, we can be sure that women were concerned about the children—those of others as well as their own. The liturgy was conducive to the action of *all* gathered; thus, children were not only welcomed, but were active participants as well. This concern for inclusiveness perhaps continued to flow in the bloodstream of African women who shared the responsibility of nurturing children at all times.

Identifiable liturgical acts uniquely shaped in the invisible institution with the input of women include the singing of songs shaped musically and textually out of the moment, reflecting an understanding of a creating God at work in the midst of the stuff of slave existence; a time of inquiry to determine (briefly) the status of the health of members of the community; prayers of invocation, petition, thanksgiving, intercession, and supplication, reflective of African people; testimonies to God's presence and intervention in the trials and tribulations of life; and confessions of personal sinful natures that had been transformed through divine intervention, with statements of intentions and commitment to live changed lives. A time of praise to God for all that God had done to keep them safe would often intensify emotions and precipitate the shouting and dancing of some of the people.

Language of the Liturgy

All ritual is communication; thus, ritual speaks through both verbal and non-verbal means. For African-Americans, in addition to the symbols of sound, words, music, moans, groans, hums, and cries, there is significant evidence from the early period of slavery that the religious song shaped by the community, both in the *koinonia* and the *diakonia*, reflect the inclusion of women. Both women and men were included in exhortations and words of caution and advice. For example, in "I'm a'Rolling Through an Unfriendly World," the line "Oh, brother, won't you help me to pray" is followed by "Oh, sister, won't you help me to pray." A few additional examples of the inclusiveness in lines from spirituals follow:

* "I Will Trust in the Lord" includes the lines, "Sister, will you trust . . ." and "Brother, will you trust . . ."

* "Scandalize My Name" includes the lines, "I met my sister . . ." and "I met my brother . . ."

* "Roll Jordan Roll" includes the lines, "Oh, Brothers, you ought t'have been there" and "Oh Sisters, you ought t'have been there."

* "Old Ship Of Zion" includes the lines, "It was good for my dear mother . . ." and "It was good for my dear father . . ." ". . . sister" and ". . . brother."

* "City Called Heaven" includes the line, "My brothers and sisters won't own me . . ."

* "I Stood on de Ribber ob Jerdon" includes the lines, "O sister, ya bettuh be ready. . ." and "Brother, ya bettuh be ready. . ."

* "The Heavenly Road" includes the alternate stanzas,
"Come, my brudder /sister, if you never did pray,
I hope you may pray tonight;
For I believe I'm a child of God
As I walk de heavenly road."

* "Nobody Knows the Trouble I See, Lord!" includes the lines, "Brothers, will you pray for me . . ." and "Sisters, will you pray for me . . ."

* "Standing in the Need of Prayer" includes the line, "Not my sister, not my brother, but it's me, O Lord."

* "De Ol' Ark's a-Moverin'" includes the lines, "See dat sistuh dressed so fine? She ain't got religion on her min(d)" and "See dat brudder dressed so gay? Satan goin' come an' carry him away."

These and many other examples also confirm the plural implication of the use of the personal pronoun "I" in so many of the African-American spirituals. While some spirituals refer to man in the English generic sense of both male and female (such as "Great Day" in the line "We want no cowards in our band . . . We call for valiant hearted men . . ."), there is clear evidence of the affirmation of African-American men in certain roles.

"He's Got the Whole World in His Hands" would probably be referenced as an example of non-inclusive God language. One must be cautious, however, when speculating about the use of masculine pronouns in songs that evolved during slavery. A strong, positive male image was surely needed to counter the negative image of the slave "master." Many African cultures refer to God as either male or female, and this image of God who is stronger, better, and wiser than the slave master could have been needed by both males and females. In most cultures it is the male to whom one looks for physical strength and protection, whether real or symbolic. Realistically, it is likely that what appears to be a generic use of the word man might have referred to the slavemaster, whose negative image and actions certainly affected the African-American male image. One such example is "God is a God, God don't never change," where the unchangeable nature of God provides confidence that there is at least one man who loves and cares enough to protect his whole creation. Other examples that can be cited are: "God is so good . . . He's so good to me"; "Mah God is so high . . . He's so low . . . an' He fills ma heart wid His love;" and "Live a-Humble" which includes "Ever see such a man as God? He gave up His Son for to come and die, just to save my soul."

In the spiritual "Ride on, King Jesus," the words "no man can a-hinder me" could certainly have been a reminder that the slavemaster was not in control of everything, least of all the ultimate freedom of the slave! Jesus, God incarnate, remains in ultimate control of things that really matter. Slaves often referred to God and Jesus interchangeably in songs.

This also provides some hint of the numerous male references to God.

Nevertheless, many non-inclusive songs from the western tradition made their way into African-American liturgy and continue to perpetuate not only sexism and classism, but racism as well. A few well-loved examples about God and Jesus Christ that are still sung with much fervor in many African-American congregations include:

* "God Will Take Care of You" has a recurring reminder that "He will take care of you."

* "My Father Is Rich" reminds the singer that God holds the wealth of this world in His hand and moves on to emphasize: "I'm a child of the King."

* "Throw Out the Life Line," with its strong sexist reference to the need of the brother and man, is also replete with racist references to darkness.

* "Have Thine Own Way, Lord" includes the phrase, "Whiter than snow, Lord, wash me just now."

* "Whiter Than Snow" also is a strong admonition to be washed whiter than snow.

* "What Can Wash Away My Sin?" has a reminder of the power of the blood to wash one white as snow.

* "Whispering Hope," a favorite during the mid-twentieth century, reminds the Black singers that hope "rends the dark veil for the soul."

Like their nineteenth-century counterparts, African-American male preachers and leaders of worship walked "well" in the ways of sexist liturgical leaders. This is not to assume that their language would have been more inclusive naturally without Euro-American exposure, but it does confirm the fact that African-American women were exposed to and subjected to male-dominated symbols and language in worship by their newly Americanized African-American fathers and brothers. What helped, however, was the courageous "womanish" women who provided at least the symbolic language of female leadership. No doubt, African-American women preachers, extending from the late eighteenth and early nineteenth century, by their mere presence and active leadership sensitized the women to the creative activity of God through females. While there is no extant data to support a concern for inclusive language, there is some evidence of ways that women have perceived and responded to religious rituals differently from men.

Ritual Behavior of African-American Women

One of the earliest ritual behaviors of women is that of naming, or more specifically, defining themselves, and maintaining that self-defined identity. Regardless of the particular familial or group environment, there is a tendency for young girls to "claim their identity," especially in the socialization process with their peers. One common ritual I observed during my own childhood was the periodic repeating or singing of one's name during solitary play. Group singing games, during which a person was invited to the center of the activity by the calling of her name, were favorites among the young girls. To mispronounce one's name evoked a visible expression of discontent and a barrage of verbal reminders of the importance of accurate pronunciation.

Long before my exposure to liturgical matters, I became aware of my own self-identity in a loving, caring, closely knit family. In a manner similar to that of some African cultures, the names that we were given connected us with the larger, extended family. There were no attempts to force us to mimic our namesake. However, we were reminded that we "belonged" in a connected way to those who had preceded us. The African concept undergirding ritual behavior at this and other levels of development is derived from the adage, "I am, because we are; and because we are, therefore, I am."[4] Belongingness remains a vital factor in all ritual behavior. While this concept transcends sexual boundaries, women are generally the carriers and perpetuators of this tradition.

Liturgical acts of nurture and protection are generally noticeable in women of all ages during worship. While some may be learned behavior, it is generally the girls who assume nurturing roles for infants and children who remain in worship. As monitors of the actions of younger children, it is not unusual to see the girls whisper words of caution, advice, and comfort directly into the ears of children for whom they have assumed the mothering task. One can observe a youthful "parent" giving directions throughout the service to the doll or teddy bear that she has brought. Although some of this behavior may subside during adolescent years, young women continue to demonstrate the actions that have been assumed by the older women.

Women are sources of liturgical healing. It is usually a woman who forces open wounds of pain in individuals so that healing can occur. It is usually a woman who helps facilitate reconciliation among members. Women are prone to keep their fingers on the pulse of the congregation and are able to find the source of trouble so that direct action to alleviate problems can take place. This gift lends itself to the provision of liturgical hospitality, which is vital in African-American worship.

There often evolves among the women a very significant role of measuring and registering the degree or quality of spirituality in the worship service. Due to her unique spiritual gifts, a woman earns this right over a period of time, and receives the name "Aunt Jane," (pronounced "A'nt Jane"), which is also a historical title for such a person. George Ofori-atta-Thomas, an authority on African traditional religions, identifies the role of Aunt Jane as a continuum of traditional African specialists, or mediums:

> In the traditional African worship, women have been the Mediums through whom the special dispensations of powers have erupted and flowed. Mediums functioned to facilitate the communication with the spirit world . . . As the spirit deepened, possession came; they were "caught up" in the spirit and became unself-conscious, and the characteristics of behavior could change . . . in another dimension of spiritual powers in control of the worship service.[5]

In worship services where traditional emotional African-American liturgical activity takes place, "Aunt Jane," like the medium, serves as an intermediary through whom a higher level of spiritual power can be released into the corporate community. A woman who has earned this position often initiates the appropriate dialogical response of the community to the words of the preacher.

As a "spiritual thermometer," she is privileged to caution the preacher aloud to "come on and say what you need to say!" Her prodding helps establish the spiritual readiness of both the preacher and the community, which can "embellish the quality of emotional tones in the worship experience."[6] Official "Aunt Janes" in contemporary African-American worship are usually devout women who serve as foundations for the spiritual momentum, both in the gathered and scattered community. Once she is identified, it is not unusual for pastors to shape their sermons and liturgical leadership so that they meet the needs of Aunt Jane.[7]

Although many liturgical actions which we now identify as sexist tended earlier to prohibit the involvement of women as pastors or liturgists, women assumed these roles with great care and commitment. As a "deaconess," "stewardess," or "mother of the church," a woman can handle the holy vessels, covers for the communion table, paraments, and flowers, as well as assist with preparation and follow-up of baptisms. Her tasks of preparing and undressing the table and assisting children and adults who are to be baptized are assumed with feminine grace and dignity.

All these roles warrant her a special place and special respect among the parishioners and the local community. The preparations necessary prior to the service also extended her tasks beyond the liturgical space of the church. Communion covers were required to be washed spotlessly white, carefully starched, and hung to dry (most often in the sun).[8] After ironing, there were to be only the natural creases of the folds. The glass communion cups were washed and sterilized to avoid the transmission of germs. The preparation of communion bread was often undertaken with great care by a deaconess or other women of the church.

There is no doubt that these responsibilities were related to the woman's role as housekeeper and cook. Nevertheless, women appreciated opportunities to be useful in matters of service and liturgical leadership. Without complaint, these roles remain a high priority for women who make a historical and spiritual connection between tasks that are in the domain of women and "things that men do" in church.

Community concerns and/or announcements are often handled by women in African-American congregations. This requires special oratory skills, a winsome personality, and familiarity with members of the congregation. Where women are still not allowed to enter the chancel space, one also needs a large dose of humility to subject one's self to a designated space "below" the pulpit, so as not to confuse the position of authority with simple acts of responsibility. This trend, though decreasing, has helped women to combine humility and authority as they respond to their call from God to a life of ordained service.

After the earlier periods when women preached, with and without ordination, women continued to seek official authorization from their denominational bodies. With the exception of a few denominations, authorization has been granted, but struggles of approval continue to exist. From the cadre of woman clergy, we note liturgical leadership styles reflecting a combination of all of the historical roles which women assumed and those to which they were assigned. The implication from this data is that women bring to the liturgical task high levels of creativity, intuition, openness to the leading of the Holy Spirit, and wholeness.

The list which follows evolved over a period of time in my seminary worship classes, workshops on worship in local churches, and personal responses, and reflects input from both women and men.

* Women have a more teaching-nurturing style of preaching.

* Women are willing to deal with the more difficult issues of life. They are less prone to "bridle the biblical text," willing to allow the text to speak to contemporary needs.

* Women are less prone to yield to pressures placed upon them by parishioners in terms of *what* is preached.

* Mannerisms during the baptism of infants reflect a special tenderness (not necessarily absent from the actions of men), revealing the sensitivity of a womb-bearer returning the child to the womb of the baptismal waters.

* The handling of the elements of the Lord's Supper is usually a combination of the mannerisms of a woman who has prepared food for her family and now hands it forth as an offering of the results of hours of labor for the fulfillment of those who have come out of their hunger to eat, with the same gentleness that Jesus offers his own body and blood to those who are to be spiritually nourished.

* Women are very likely to look the recipient of the elements of communion directly in the eye, as if to assure the communicant that the spiritual food is not of human creation.

* Women are willing to dare to take risks that will enhance the spiritual life of the congregation.

* Women are more prone to keep meaningful rituals alive and to introduce new rituals that allow the congregations to experience new levels of nurture and growth—e.g., renewal of baptismal vows, altering procedures for performing rituals, relating ritual action to actions in the daily life of the community.

* Women are prone to become actively involved in the work of women's organizations, without assuming highly visible leadership roles.

* In addition to welcoming persons to assume quasi-parental roles or to serve as endorsers of their decisions, good or bad, women also tend to develop and maintain personal friendships with some congregants.

* Women are free to avoid liturgical actions that negate any person in the liturgy; women are more prone to admit their errors, ask forgiveness, and make corrections, even during the worship service.

* With a concern for the subjective, intuitive, feeling (instead of simply objective-rational thinking), women are free to incorporate opportunities for touching, reflecting, and meditating.

* Touching and laying on of hands during worship connects with the woman's natural manner of employing soothing, healing touch in other aspects of life, especially as related to the nurturing of children.

Future Projections

Liturgical renewal is needed among African-Americans, not only to correct historical errors, but to move the liturgical community faithfully and obediently into the future. This can be done out of an awareness that ritual action in the liturgy is created by humans, and more specifically the gathered worshiping community, and, therefore, must be contextualized. This can be done as the community of faith recognizes that symbolic representations of encounters with God are reflective of culture, yet transcend cultures. This means that there may be some actions that transcend what one might assume is expected of people merely because they are African-American.

Liturgical renewal, while acknowledging the fallacies of racism, sexism, and classism, must seek ways to open these wounds for healing, move beyond criticizing those who are guilty of these acts, and listen for and heed divine directions. Specifics that will facilitate renewal include the following:

* Affirmation of an African-American spirituality which can speak directly to African-American women.

* Dialogue with African women to determine more direct roots of liturgical actions unique to African-American women.

* Dialogue among African-American women, both lay and clergy, which can help focus directions for liturgical renewal.

* Incorporation of the stories and struggles of women in general, and African-American women in particular, in the liturgical tradition of the church.

* Publication of materials that will provide both an interdenominational and ecumenical focus of liturgical action.

* Encouraging professors of homiletics and worship to explore alternative liturgical possibilities with their female students. Encourage women to concentrate in liturgy and theology, and to provide leadership in the developing of what could be called a "womanist liturgical tradition."

As we move into the future, African-American women who provide liturgical leadership, whether as laity or ordained clergy, should be clear and honest about the reality of how they perceive themselves as women in leadership roles. African-American women will continue to face resistance as they assume roles historically reserved for others, and must be willing to remain true to themselves as they cultivate trusting relationships. Renita Weems' observation is quite accurate: "one of the best ways to get an idea of how a woman feels about being a woman is to take a look at how she treats other women."[9] Experiences of solidarity that come from participating honestly and trustingly with women and men will allow the church to become the whole church that it claims to be, without the barriers that normally divide us.

Liturgical renewal demands that our engagement beyond the worship environment be consistent with our participation in worship. God calls us in Jesus Christ to rejoice in hope, be patient in suffering, persevere in prayer, contribute to the needs of the saints, extend hospitality to strangers, live in harmony with one another, and allow love to be genuine. Renewed and renewing liturgical engagement must empower persons to live as they worship.

Notes

1. Alice Walker, *The Color Purple* (New York: Harcourt, Brace, and Jovanovich, 1983) xi.

2. Jacqueline Grant, "Womanist Theology: Black Women's Experiences as a Source for Doing Theology, with Special References to *African American Religious Studies: An Interdisciplinary Anthology*, ed. Gayraud S. Wilmore (Durham: Duke University Press, 1989) 213.

3. See especially Eric H. Erikson, "Ontogeny of Ritualization in Man," in *Philosophical Transactions of the Royal Society of London*, Series B, no. 772, vol. CCLI (1966) 337-350; and Erving Goffman, *Interaction Ritual: Essays on Face-to-Face Behavior* (Garden City: Doubleday, 1967).

4. John S. Mbiti, *African Religions and Philosophy* (Garden City: Anchor Books, Doubleday, 1970) 141.

5. George Ofori-atta-Thomas, "The African Inheritance in the Black Church Worship," in Melva Wilson Costen and Darius Swann, eds., *The Black Christian Worship Experience*, rev. and enlarged ed. (Atlanta: The ITC Press, 1992) 55.

6. Ibid. 56.

7. The writer affirms this historical legendary figure by reminding seminary students that there may be a "new Aunt Jane" serving as a conduit through which the Holy Spirit is manifested in worship. She could be an active or retired holder of an advanced academic degree, who combines her natural spiritual gifts with her desire for depth and substance in both the sermon and in liturgical action. This is to help alleviate the desire of those who would direct their sermons and leadership simply in an effort to encourage empty, "unbridled emotionalism" without substance.

8. Communion covers dried in the sun, according to church women of my youth, added the blessings of the Son of Righteousness.

9. Renita J. Weems, *Just A Sister Away* (San Diego: LuraMedia, 1988) x.

2

"She Was Born to be Powerful": The Witch and the Virgin Mary in Isthmus Zapotec Belief Narratives

Dana Everts-Boehm

RESEARCHERS OF FOLK RELIGION THEORIZE THAT THE BELIEF IN FE-male spirits can be understood as a projection of female status in society onto the supernatural realm. And in the supernatu-ral realm cross-culturally, there are few positive female role models, according to many ethnographers. Folklorist Kay Turner writes that "women have been denied their right to im-ages which define and promote female power and indepen-dence."[1] Anthropologists Rosaldo and Lamphere postulate that in many cultures women are excluded from participation in religious ritual because they are conceived to be inherently earth-bound and non-spiritual.[2] Moreover, some scholars argue that even in societies where sacred female images are prevalent, these images have been co-opted by the patriarchal power structure to validate male domination. According to Marina Warner, adulation of the Virgin Mary in Mediterrane-an Catholic cultures reinforces female subordination by pre-senting women with a role model who advocates self-denial and submission to male authority.[3]

Negative female images, on the other hand, reportedly abound cross-culturally. Clare Garrett writes that "in nearly every society that believes in witches, the vast majority of suspects are women."[4] Scholars postulate that in male-dominated cultures female power is categorically associated with witchcraft. That is, any woman who is perceived as powerful is automatically suspected of having attained her power through supernatural, malevolent means.[5]

As ethnographic work becomes increasingly sensitive to the female contribution to culture, it is clear that the relationship between female spirits and women's status in society is more complex and multivalent than earlier studies might suggest. This paper examines traditional folk belief in negative and positive female entities, as expressed through belief narratives, revealing how these entities are interpreted differently by men and women in their ongoing dialectic over power and gender.

Preliminary evidence suggests that even in patriarchal societies, men and women have alternative, conflicting interpretations of female spiritual beings. Unless data expressing the female perspective is elicited and studied, scholars are left to interpret culture solely through male eyes. The fact that the male side of culture has been more thoroughly researched than the female side accounts for a marked tendency in ethnographic, literary, and even feminist research to depict women as reacting to, rather than creating, culture—as the recipients of male ideology rather than the builders of their own ideology.

My data is collected from the Isthmus Zapotec community of Juchitán in southern Oaxaca, during my sojourn there in the years 1981-1983. This Mexican Indian culture evinces both a vital belief in female witches, called *bidxaa* in the Isthmus Zapotec language, and an equally strong belief in local manifestations of the Virgin Mary. From the male perspective, witches engender social divisiveness, whereas the Virgin Mary creates social harmony. Women, however, talk about both the Virgin Mary and the witch as protectors of female interests.

The second largest city in Oaxaca, Juchitán has a population of about seventy thousand, eighty percent of whom are Zapotec Indians. Juchitán is located on the Isthmus of Tehuantepec near the Pacific Coast; hence the people are called "Isthmus

Zapotec" to distinguish them from the Valley and Mountain Zapotec. The Isthmus Zapotec culture is noted for the high status of women.[6] Virtually all of the ethnographic data on this society remarks on the bold, independent, commercially astute character of the women. Stereotyped as a matriarchy by many Mexicans, the Isthmus Zapotec are rather a remarkably egalitarian society in which men and women share power. Isthmus Zapotec women control the local market, finance and organize the fiesta system, and as a rule, work outside of the home. Many, in fact, are traveling saleswomen, going as far as Mexico City to sell hammocks, gold jewelry, dried shrimp, and other goods.

The issue of female versus male power is nonetheless a hot one which openly concerns both sexes. Aware that most of Mexico thinks they are dominated by women, Isthmus Zapotec men are quick to point out to visitors that women do *not* run the town, as they do not hold political office. Yes, they work outside the home and organize the fiestas, but these activities generate income and status for their families. Men often state that they are, in fact, proud of the industrious Isthmus Zapotec women. But they explain that these freedoms are *allowed* by men only insofar as they positively impact family and social life.

Women are less complimentary when the subject is Isthmus Zapotec men—which it often is. They openly criticize male behavior, citing physical violence, jealousy, adultery, alcoholism, and child neglect as inherently male problems which adversely impact family life. Women clearly articulate the concept that the sexes have different, often opposing spheres of interest, and they do not hesitate to champion the female sphere when conflicts occur. A frequent boast of the Zapotec woman is that she "sabe pelear" ("knows how to fight").

A marked divergence of thought is particularly noticeable in comparing the way men and women talk about witches. Contrast the following four descriptions of the same person—a woman widely reputed to be a witch. The first descriptions are from two young men in their mid-twenties, Andrés and Roberto. These are followed by an excerpt of a conversation between two women also in their twenties, Chica and Faustina.[7]

Male Descriptions of the Witch

Account 1: Andrés
They called her Luisa Saltillo. She used to sell pots. But she also dedicated herself to that work, the work of the *bidxaa*. And she aged before her time. When she was fifty she looked eighty. She had only three teeth left, and you could see them when she talked or laughed. And she was very evil.

Account 2: Roberto
Luisa Saltillo used to sell pots. And they say that she used to transform herself into a *bidxaa*. She'd change herself into a cow or a bull. She liked to suck the blood of babies. She worked at night. She'd go out to suck their blood, then return home. Everyone knew she was very fierce, very violent.

Female Descriptions of the Witch

Account 3: Chica and Faustina
Chica: María Luisa used to sell pots. She was a witch. Everyone used to say that.
Faustina: They say that she used to change into a pig or some other animal, but that she never did anything. She never harmed anyone for money.
Chica: She scared me, though. Because if you went up to buy something from her and only asked the price, she'd get mad. She'd start to say things to you, she'd bother you.
Faustina: She never bothered me. When I passed by her, we'd talk, and she never did anything to me.

Both men and women state that this individual, María Luisa Saltillo, is a witch. But whereas the men describe her as "evil" and "violent," the women depict her as an irascible character in the marketplace who practices a hard sell. To Andrés and Roberto, Luisa Saltillo is a toothless fiend who turns into a bull and sucks the blood of infants. To Chica and Faustina, María Luisa is an eccentric old woman who is essentially harmless, even if she *does* transform herself into a pig from time to time. Faustina asserts that she was never paid to harm anyone. From the female perspective, her chief fault is that she is an overly aggressive saleswoman—a trait which, by the way, is attributed to *most* Isthmus Zapotec market women by outsiders unaccustomed to their forthright manner.

The folk belief complex of the Isthmus Zapotec *bidxaa* (witch) includes the following motifs, which appear frequently in witch narratives:[8]

1. The witch is usually female. When a male witch occurs in a narrative, he is usually a partner of the female witch.

2. The witch goes out at night, removes her clothing, and turns into an animal such as a pig, a cow, a cat, a dog, a monkey, a horse, or a rat.

3. In animal form she sucks the blood of fetuses and infants, causing miscarriages and infant death. She also chases men at night, running between their legs, tripping them, and jumping up and down on them, leaving terrible bruises on their bodies as physical evidence of her attack.

4. She contracts her services for pay. Witchcraft is thought to be a profession. The witch is hired to attack, intimidate and often kill people—generally babies and men.

5. The ability to turn oneself into an animal is inherited, not learned.

6. The witch can be captured by being struck with a belt soaked in human urine. This forces her to return to her human form. In the stories it is invariably a man who attempts to capture a witch; and in many cases the witch persuades him to let her go by implying sexual favors (she is naked when she returns to human form) and/or because she offers him money.[9]

Interestingly, local witch narratives contend that those who hire witches are invariably women. The chief motivation cited for hiring a *bidxaa* is to prevent one's husband or lover from romancing another woman or, failing that, to prevent the other woman from bearing his child. A typical scenario is this: a woman's husband has an extramarital affair. The wife contracts a witch to chase the husband at night, either to prevent him from reaching the house of his mistress or to punish him for having spent the night with her. If the affair continues and the mistress becomes pregnant or has a baby, the wife contracts a witch to kill the child in hopes that the child's death will destroy the bond between her husband and his mistress.

The following account told by Andrés illustrates this pattern. The story, which Andrés heard from his mother, tells of a witch's attack on his father. Andrés was illegitimate: his mother was his father's mistress. The legitimate wife allegedly paid her relatives, who were witches, to punish Andrés' father for his extramarital affair.

Account 4: Andrés

My father left my mother's house early one morning on his way home. And then he saw something rolling straight towards him. When he tried to pass by it, it turned into a pig. And the pig went between his legs and if he hadn't put his feet far apart it would have knocked him down. When he turned to see the pig it wasn't there anymore—it had disappeared. And when the sun came up, he looked between his legs and they were badly bruised. They say this was done by his wife's relatives.

Andrés added that his father's wife's relatives killed his mother's first born child by sucking the baby's blood at night. The same witch then attempted unsuccessfully to kill Andrés shortly after his birth, but he survived because his mother decided to fight fire with fire: she hired another witch, the aforementioned María Luisa Saltillo, to guard him.

Account 5: Andrés

In this story, which qualifies as a legend proper—a fully formed narrative more distantly related to an experiential base—Andrés tells of a newly married wife who "dedicated herself to this line of work" (his own wording). One night her suspicious husband follows her and observes her disrobe, hide her clothes, and roll around on the ground until she transforms into a cow. When she runs off he confiscates her clothes and shows them to her parents. Restored to human form, she returns naked at dawn to find her husband and parents awaiting her. Her father "beats her until she is half dead." Her husband tells her, "Why should I continue with you if you dedicate yourself to this line of work? We wouldn't be happy together. We should separate." The man remarries while the witch remains single, aging rapidly and dying while still young. Andrés ends the story with the comment, "Maybe that was her punishment for having done harm to certain people."

In the male accounts the *bidxaa* is characterized as a woman perversely devoted to her unusual profession, which is described both as an avocation and a vice. The woman who "dedicates herself to this work" thereby threatens family life— both the families of others and her own family. Andrés and

Roberto explain that witches abort their own babies in the process of transforming themselves into animals; and of course they are held responsible for killing other people's babies as well. And the witch alienates her husband, eventually bringing about a divorce. The violence inflicted on the witch by a male (usually a father or husband) is rationalized as an attempt at correcting her evil proclivities. In Andrés' story, the witch refuses to abandon her profession even after being beaten and threatened with divorce. Roberto's very similar story has a different ending.

Account 6: Roberto
And her husband grabbed her and beat her very badly. He hit her hard. After that, she quit doing it. Now she has children, she doesn't abort them anymore.

The belief narratives about witches that are told by women differ significantly from male accounts in the following ways:

1. The witch is invariably a real person—a neighbor, a relative, a market woman—with whom the narrator, or an associate, has had personal contact.

2. The accounts focus on how the alleged witch uses her unusual skills strategically in every day situations to achieve practical ends; capriciously, for the sheer pleasure of exercising power; or judiciously, to punish the unjust, protect the innocent, or teach a lesson.

3. The motif of the man punishing the female witch is absent.

Another striking difference lies in the tone of the storytelling. Both male narrators adopted a stern, didactic manner while talking about the *bidxaa*. The women's stories, on the other hand, were frequently punctuated by laughter, and were clearly enjoyed as a form of light entertainment. The following account told by Chica illustrates both the tone and the characteristics of witch narratives related by women. Chica told this story to an all-female gathering including her cousin Angela, her friend Faustina, folklorist Tina Bucuvalas, and myself.

Account 7: Chica
This guy had a friend who was a barmaid. And one time they were talking about this, about witches. And she herself was one of them (laughs). So the girl said she knew something about this. Well, the boy didn't believe her. Then she said to him that she would show him, if he wouldn't be afraid of her.

"But if you're afraid," she says, "I won't show you." "How could I be afraid of you when you're a woman and I'm a man?" says the boy. "How *could* you scare me?" "Okay," she says, "but I guarantee you're going to be scared of me" (laughs). "No, I won't be," says the boy. Then everybody saw her do somersaults around and around and turn into a dog, a dog, a *dog*! (laughs). And the dog ran over and nipped at the boy's foot. Yes, she scared him! He took off—he didn't stick around (laughs). And they say that he hid inside of a neighbor woman's crate. They say that he lost his mind. She *did* scare him, so much that he went crazy! (laughs).

The themes present in Chica's account are evident in other stories told by Chica and Faustina. One story centers on how a market woman uses her reputation as a witch to frighten customers into paying higher prices for her wares, and to intimidate other market women into selling to her at a lower rate. Another account reports how a monkey, found in a neighbor's tamarind tree, was thought to be the neighbor woman herself in animal form. Chica also talked about her father's sister-in-law who is said to be a witch. Chica explained that, being a witch, the sister-in-law could not bear children; so she adopted a nephew, raised him well, and paid for his education. Now the nephew is married and has his own house. "Es buena gente" ("She's a good person"), Chica said of the reputed witch.

The male view of witches reveals an uneasiness about female independence and solidarity. As previously noted, Isthmus Zapotec women generally work outside of the home, organize and participate in the fiesta system, often maintaining financial and social independence from their husbands. All this is accepted by men with the stipulation that these activities benefit the family. The male portrait of the *bidxaa* is that of female independence run amuck—the woman as home-wrecker. Hired to attack someone else's children and spouse, aborting her own babies and those of others, alienating her husband to the point of divorce, the *bidxaa* destroys family life because she is too "dedicated to her work"—a phrase which is uttered frequently in the male accounts. Moreover, men suspect that women do not condemn the witch as they do, but secretly emulate her. Andrés assumes that all women would be tempted to acquire the powers of a witch if they could. Asked if witchcraft is thought to be learned or inherited, he replied, "It must be natural (inherited). Because if it was learned, imagine how many witches there would be! They would invade the entire city. All their children, grandchildren, everyone would learn it!"

In contrast, the female portrait of the witch is ambiguous, complex, ultimately human. The witch is depicted as a real person whom one knows and even talks to, rather than an anonymous blood-sucking fiend. The witch is a market woman, a neighbor, an in-law, even "buena gente"—a "good person." Some of these witches frighten other woman (like the potter who scared Chica) while others inspire amusement (like the barmaid who turned into a dog). These female narrators perceive witches as persons much like themselves, except that they have access to special powers.

The grim belief that witches cause miscarriages and infant death is actually useful to women as a tool to dissuade their husbands from having extramarital affairs.[10] If a woman miscarries or her baby becomes ill, the witch belief complex allows her to blame it on her philandering husband, arguing that his mistress has hired a witch to eliminate his legitimate children. The husband is charged with endangering his offspring through his own careless indiscretion. The wife's tendency to blame her husband rather than the female rival is reflected by the absence of any reference to a witch harming an adult woman in the narratives. Rather than paying a witch to attack her husband's mistress, the wronged wife—according to local belief legends—traditionally hires a witch to punish her husband. Functionally, then, there *is* a real solidarity between women and witches in the sense that women use the witch belief complex to influence male behavior, rather than to criticize or punish other women.

The witch can even serve as a positive role model for Isthmus Zapotec women. I know of one case in which a self-proclaimed *bidxaa* achieved widespread public acclaim. The potter described earlier—Na Luisa Saltillo—became so well-known in Juchitán that the section of town where she lived was named after her. The people of "Saltillo" (officially named "Santa Cruz de Cheguigo") felt that they benefitted from Na Luisa's power and her presence in their community. It was reported that people *did* actually contract her services as a witch, in spite of Faustina's assertion to the contrary. And Chica implied that her success in the market may be related to the fact that some people were afraid *not* to buy her pots. However she attained it, the important thing is that she shared her wealth with her neighbors by becoming a godparent to many children and sponsoring local fiestas. Her allegedly ill-gotten gains enriched her community, and so she became a prominent citizen in her part of town.

The Virgin Mary, another female image prevalent in the Isthmus Zapotec belief system, is, unlike the witch, an unequivocally positive model. Local beliefs about the Virgin indicate how a patriarchally organized religion, such as Catholicism, can be significantly reshaped into a folk religion with a substantial shift of worship from a god to a goddess.

The Virgin Mary is so revered in Juchitán that in some instances she usurps the customary position of God. One example is the local adulation of "la Mano Poderosa," "The Powerful Hand." A standard image from Catholic iconography, "The Powerful Hand" appears in the form of cheap prints sold in markets all over Mexico. The print illustrates a huge hand in the sky with the words "La Mano Poderosa" underneath it. According to the local priests, this image depicts the hand of God. Disregarding the priests' opinion, as they so often do, Isthmus Zapotecs believe that "La Mano Poderosa" is the hand of Mary. They further believe that Mary's Hand is periodically incarnated locally in the form of a plant. At least three local Powerful Hands in the guise of trees or branches were recognized in Juchitán from 1981-1983.[11]

The Powerful Hand with the largest and most fervent following during this time was located in Cheguigu, the eighth section of Juchitán. A small tree with five branches stretched out like fingers, it was sheltered by an outdoor latticework chapel built especially for it, in which it receives a steady stream of petitioners year round. Na Flore, a flower seller from Cheguigu, told me how this particular incarnation of the Virgin Mary was discovered. I recorded this narrative while visiting her in the flower market one day.

Account 8: Na Flore
A woman planted her. She grew in the shape of a hand with five branches, like that. Her neighbor had a dream that she

[the tree] told her [the neighbor] that her name was María. "I'm a woman," she says. She spoke like a little girl about seven or eight years old. "I already told my mother, but she ignores me. She says it isn't true," she says, "but my name *is* María and I need a *rezo* [prayer meeting]." So the neighbor went to the woman's house. "Yes, it's true," she says, "I have a sapling. It's growing in the shape of a hand. I dreamed about it too, and it told me "Mama, my name is María. I am below this house. I am here and I look like a hand." But she didn't pay any attention to her, she didn't speak to her [the tree]. When the neighbor came over that day, she finally realized that she really had a Hand, that there was a Hand there. "I am María," she said. She was born to be powerful.

Having realized that a Powerful Hand was growing in her yard, the woman promptly cleared away plants surrounding it and enshrined it in an elaborate latticework chapel. The tree was about four feet high when I visited it. Its trunk was painted white and its five branches did resemble a hand. The tree was surrounded by vases of flowers and candles. A delicate white arch framed it and from this arch dangled numerous *milagros*, gold necklaces and crosses bearing the name "María." These are the gifts petitioners have brought in return for cures and favors believed granted by the Hand.

Once the chapel was built, word began to spread that a new incarnation of Holy Mary was growing across the river in Cheguigu. People began to dream that the tree was telling them to come and visit it. Now every year, the tree is given a *rezo* (prayer meeting) on 22 February, the day its "mother" acknowledged its status as a holy being. Its many visitors ask the Powerful Hand for cures and other favors and "siempre cumple su promesa" ("she always keeps her promise"). Those who are granted their petition sometimes pay for a Mass in the church in honor of the Powerful Hand. (It is customary for petitioners making a request of a holy being to promise something in return, whether it be a Mass, a prayer gathering, a gold necklace, or an embroidered cloth.) The officiating priest is not aware that he is celebrating a Mass for a tree, as he is told simply that it is for the Virgin Mary.

According to Na Flore and the other women I asked, most of the Powerful Hand's petitioners are women. They say that the Hand specializes in safe pregnancies and births. Pregnant women visiting the tree in Cheguigu scoop up some of the melted wax from votive candles placed around it. They wrap the wax up in a wilted blossom or leaf from one of the bouquets surrounding it and take it home with them. The wax is later used as an ointment to massage the pregnant woman's stomach during labor.

* * * * * *

The witch and the Powerful Hand both function as vehicles to express and further female interests.[12] The Powerful Hand is particularly adept at ensuring safe pregnancies and childbirth. Yet while the witch is held responsible for miscarriages and infant deaths, she can also be called upon to protect babies from other witches. One example is the aforementioned instance in which the infamous pottery seller, Luisa Saltillo, was hired to protect Andrés from another witch when he was a baby.

Account 9: Andrés
They paid this woman, Na Luisa Saltillo, to come and guard me. She came in the form of a big cat. They paid her 250 pesos to guard me for several days. That's how I got well.

Even the witch can contribute to a child's well being, for a price. Of course the Powerful Hand is also paid for her cures and protection in the form of gold necklaces and embroidered cloths bearing her name, as well as prayer meetings and Masses held in her honor. A major distinction between these two beings is that the witch symbolizes female power in opposition to the will of men—specifically in the areas of work, marriage, and reproduction—whereas the Powerful Hand acts as a sort of supernatural midwife.

Because the Virgin Mary in the form of the Powerful Hand benefits women's interests within the socially acceptable frame of childbearing, she is regarded by men as a purely benevolent female holy being. Yet Isthmus Zapotec women see witches too as protectors of female interests, albeit those interests which may conflict with men. Witches symbolize female independence of thought and action: the desire to work outside of the home, to devote oneself to a profession; the choice of whether to bear, or not to bear, children; the urge to curtail a husband's extramarital affairs, to make him accept responsibility for the welfare of his children; and, finally, the basic wish to be powerful. The alleged witch is thought to be the woman's ally in these areas; and as such, she is tolerated, respected and perhaps even emulated by women at the same time that she is condemned by men. Thus, the witch also symbolizes female solidarity in the face of male opposition.

Given the gender-based difference of opinion about witches, it would be simplistic to characterize the Isthmus Zapotec *bidxaa* as either a "positive" or a "negative" female image for the culture as a whole. The fact that half the population regards the witch as ambiguous while the other half condemns her as evil suggests the possibility that perhaps what we call "Isthmus Zapotec culture" may be composed of two divergent, gender-based structures of thought.

This case study points to the need to elicit the female interpretation of culture in pursuing ethnographic inquiry. The analysis of cultural reality has hitherto tended to parallel early Greek ideas of human conception: that the sperm alone carried the blueprint for the baby and the mother was simply the nurturing environment.[13] An implicit, unexamined paradigm for cultural studies has been that culture is essentially a male construct that is imposed on women. Yet it is increasingly evident that the female contribution to social structures, ideologies and religions has been vastly underrated and overlooked. Recent linguistic research in the United States postulates that there are identifiably distinct male and female patterns of discourse. It is quite likely that these distinctions extend beyond language to other areas of culture—and not just in the United States but in many societies. Perhaps all human cultures are, in fact, composed of two world-views, two distinct male and female ideologies which, united, create a whole cultural system.

Notes

1. Kay Turner, "Mexican-American Women's Home Altars," *Lady-Unique-Inclination of the Night* (Austin: University of Texas Folklore Center, Spring, 1979) 2-4.

2. Michelle Z. Rosaldo and Louise Lamphere, *Women, Culture and Society* (Palo Alto: Stanford University Press, 1974).

3. Marina Warner, *Alone of All Her Sex: The Myth and Cult of the Virgin Mary* (New York: Alfred Knopf, Random House, 1976).

4. Clare Garrett, "Women and Witches: Patterns of Analysis," *Signs* 3: 461-470.

5. See, for example, A.D.J. MacFarlane, *Witchcraft in Tudor and Stuart England* (London: Routledge and Kegan Paul Ltd., 1970) 205, 215; S.F. Nadel, "Witchcraft in Four African Societies," *American Anthropologist* 54: 18-20; and Alan Anderson and Raymond Gordon, "Witchcraft and the Status of Women—the Case of England," *British Journal of Sociology* 29, No. 2: 171-184.

6. See Beverly Litzler Chiñas, *The Isthmus Zapotec: Women's Roles in Cultural Context* (New York: Holt, Rinehart, and Winston, 1973); Miguel Covarrubias, *Mexico South: The Isthmus of Tehuantepec* (New York: Alfred Knopf, 1967); and Anya Peterson Royce, "Prestige and Affiliation in an Urban Community: Juchitan, Oaxaca" (Ph.D. thesis, University of California-Berkeley, 1974).

7. These narratives about *bidxaa* or Isthmus Zapotec witches were tape-recorded during fieldwork for my doctorate in Juchitán, 1981-1983. Although my focus of study was not witchcraft, the subject often came up during interviews or conversations.

8. This list of motifs is based on research and my fieldwork data. Sources for Isthmus Zapotec witch narratives include Gilberto Orozco, *Tradiciones y leyendas del Istmo de Tehuántepec* (N.p.: Revistas Musical Mexicana, 1946); Beverly Litzler Chiñas, *The Isthmus Zapotec*; Miguel Covarrubias, *Mexico South*; Elsie Clews Parsons, *Mitla, Town of Souls* (Chicago: University of Chicago Press, 1936); Paul Radin, "Cuentos y leyendas de los Zapotecos," in *Tlalocan* I (Sacramento: House of Tlaloc, 1943), and Anya Peterson Royce's unpublished field notes.

9. Orozco, *Tradiciones*.

10. This idea was first suggested to me by Anya Peterson Royce in discussing her field notes about Isthmus Zapotec witches.

11. See Dana Everts, "Women Are Flowers: The Exploration of a Dominant Metaphor in Isthmus Zapotec Expressive Culture," (Bloomington: University of Indiana doctoral thesis, 1990) 369-374, for more information on the *mano poderosa* ("powerful hand") phenomenon in Juchitán.

12. Isthmus Zapotec women appear to identify very closely with both the Virgin Mary and the *bidxaa* (witch). Traditional female curers or *curanderas* invoke the power of the Virgin to cure but are also sometimes suspected of being *bidxaa* themselves. Thus, in the local belief system there is a conceptual link between the Virgin and the witch that is embodied in the personage of the *curandera;* see Everts, "Women Are Flowers" 255-256, 363.

13. This idea, Greek in origin, was inherited and supported by the medieval Christian Church, which taught that the human fetus or

"homunculus" was an entirely formed "little person" made by the male and planted in the woman during intercourse; see Barbara Ehrenreich and Deirdre English, *Witches, Midwives and Nurses: A History of Women Healers* (Old Westbury, NY: The Feminist Press, 1973) 10-11.

Appendix: Texts in Spanish

These texts were transcribed from field tapes recorded in Juchitán during the years 1981-1983. Copies of these tapes have been donated to the Archives of Traditional Music at Indiana University in Bloomington. The italicized words are in Isthmus Zapotec. Departures from standard Spanish may be attributed to the fact that Spanish is the second language for the speakers, Isthmus Zapotec being their first language.

Account 1: Andrés
Se llamaba Luisa Saltillo. Vendía ollas. Pero se dedicaba a eso trabajo de *bidxaa*. Y se puso muy vieja antes de su tiempo. Cuando ya cumplió cincuenta años, parecía tener unos ochenta años. Y ya no tenía dientes, unos trés nada más. Pero que se podía ver, pues, cuando ella hablaba, cuando se reía, sí. Y era muy mala.

Account 2: Roberto
Luisa Saltillo vendía ollas. Y ella . . . decía, pues, que ella siempre se convertía en *bidxaa*. Convertía ella en un toro o una vaca. Le gustó chupar la sangre de un niño tierno. Ella de noche es que trabajaba. Iba no más a chupar la sangre, luego regresó a su casa. Sabían que era muy atrabajada, muy terrible ella.

Account 3: Chica and Faustina
Chica: María Luisa vendía ollas, y fué bruja. La gente la conocía, lo decía eso. Mucha gente dice eso.
Faustina: Dicen que se convertía en marrano, en cualquier animal, pero nunca hacía nada. Creo que nunca hizo daño para dinero.
Chica: A mí me daba miedo de ella porque seguro que si vas a comprar algo y nada más vas a preguntar el precio, empieza a decirte algo. Le molesta, pues.
Faustina: A mí no me molestó. Cuando pasé yo, estabamos platicando, y no me hizo nada.

Account 4: Andrés
Salió de aquí (la casa de mi madre) en la madrugada, y se iba para su casa. Y ya mira, veía algo que venía revolcando derechita donde él . . . y él iba a pasar. Se formó, se transformó en un marrano, y se pasó entre las piernas, y si él no se hiciera desjuntos los pies, le iba a tirar. Y al voltear a ver al marrano, ya no estaba. Se desapareció. Y ya al amanecer, ya al hacer más claro el día, entonces vió entre las piernas, tenían morados. Bien morados, un moradote así grande. Dicen que son los mismos parientes de su esposa.

Account 5: Andrés
(Note: this is the second of two versions I taped by Andrés of the same story. It is paraphrased in the essay, but here is the story as Andrés told it.)
   Dicen que esa señora desde antes ya se dedicaba a ese trabajo. Pero cuando se casaron, su esposo no creía a la gente de que era verdad que ella tuvo ese trabajo. Una noche que su esposo pues disimulando de que ya estaba durmiendo, se levantó a seguirla, espiarla. Dicen que se iba a encontrar en un lugar donde hay las cuatro esquinas de una calle. Entonces se llegaron allí. Se empezaron a desvestirse y sus ropas las escondian en un lugar oscuro entre ladrillos. Y despues de esconder, todos desnudos se revolcaron en la arena para darse la forma de cierto animal. Ella se transformó en una vaca, y otras en cerdos, toros, cualquier animal. Entonces se salieron.
   Y el esposo, cuando vió que habian salidos, fué a sacar sus ropas y las llevó a la casa de su suegra, dando la seña de que ella se dedicaba a ese trabajo sin que sus papas se dieron cuenta. Cuando llevó la prueba de la ropa, el señor se nota que su hija se formó en ese animal. Ese señor, lo que hizo fué de ir a la casa de su hija. Fué con el esposo a esperarla. Y cuando llegó la señora, llegó desnuda. Y de allí, su papá la tuvo que pegar, hasta que dejarla media muerta. Entonces su esposo la dice, "Pues, no, para que voy a seguir contigo, si tu te dediques a ese trabajo, pues no vamos a vivir feliz. Y ahora debemos separarnos." Y así se separaron y no tuvieron hijos. El señor se casó con otra mujer. Y ella se quedó sola. Y aunque estaba joven, se puso a adevejerse, se murió ella. Será tal vez el castigo para hacer daño a ciertas personas.

Account 6: Roberto
Y le agarró a su esposa y le pegó pero bien feo. Lastimó bastante. Ya despues, dejó de hacerlo ella. Ahora ya tiene hijos, ya no aborta.

Account 7: Chica
Es que aquel muchacho tenía amiga que era cantinera. Y entonces estaban hablando de eso, de bruja. Y que esa muchacha era de esto tambien. Y le dijo la muchacha que tambien sabe de esta brujería. Entonces el muchacho, pues no lo creía, dijo que no es cierto. Entonces le dijo al muchacho que si no tenía miedeo de ella, pues entonces que le va a mostrar. "Pero si tienes miedo," le dice al muchacho, "pues no te voy a mostrar." "No," dice el muchacho, "como te voy a tener miedo si tu eres una mujer y yo soy hombre?" "Bueno," dice, "pero te aseguro que sí que me vas a tener miedo" (se rie). "No," le dijo el muchacho. Luego la gente la vió como revolcó. Y ella se volvió perro, perro, pero perro! (se rie). Y el perro iba a jalar el pie del muchacho. Pero el muchacho, sí que le dió miedo! Salió— ya no se quedó él allí (se rie). Y dice que él se metió en una caja de una vecina, allí se metió él. Volvió el muchacho como loco, dice. Que sí le dió miedo, hasta tonto se quedó!

Account 8: Na Flore
La señora lo sembró como un árbol. Se hizo como una mano, ya sacó cinco ramas así. Y cuando soñó su vecina, dice que se llama María. Es mujer, dice. Habló con su vecina en su sueño. Habló como una niña de ocho, siete años. "Ya le dije a mi mamá, pero no me hace caso," dice. "Dice que no es cierto, pero yo me llamo María, y ahora necesito un rezo." Entonces fué la vecina a buscar donde vive la señora. "Sí, es cierto," dice, "tengo un palo. Salió una mano. También me soñé y me dijo, `Mamá, yo me llamo María. Estoy debajo de esta casa,' dice, `estoy,' dice, `pero como una mano no más,' dice." Y ella no hizo caso, dice, no habló nada. Y cuando vino la vecina, ese dîa ya hizo caso la dueña de que tiene mano, de que hay mano allí. "Soy María," dice. Nació para ser poderosa, pues.

3

Twisting Space: Women, Spirits, and Halloween

Karen Sue Hybertsen

THE INVITATION, DROPPED THROUGH THE MAIL SLOT, MARKS THE BE-
ginning of a journey through time and space. The young
couple walks together through town to the appointed address
only to discover the house dark and silent. After some hesita-
tion they knock on the door. Some minutes pass, and finally
the door creaks slowly open. An eerie, feminine spirit beckons
them inside. The darkened rooms through which she leads
them are a veritable maze of cornstalks, pumpkins, and autumn foliage. The silent tour concludes in the brightly lit kitch-
en, where a fire warms the forbidding atmosphere. Gradually
other couples join them and then, when their number is complete, the spirit presents them with an array of divinatory
games for their evening's pleasure. They name nuts, set them
on the fireplace to see if they jump—a way of assessing faithfulness in their relationships. They try the challenge of the
three luggies, dishes filled with clear water, dark water, or
nothing. Their blindfolded selection denotes their marital
course in life—happy, widowhood, or never to marry. Later
they adjourn to the dining room and share cider, nuts and other foods of the night. A ghost story told round the fire concludes the evening. It is Halloween night at the turn of the
twentieth century in the United States.

* * * * * *

Halloween, as we know it today, is largely a construct of the late Victorian period. The everyday books of the period portrayed Halloween as a holiday deeply rooted in our collective pagan past. In defining the holiday, three strands of religious and ritual history were drawn together to provide a recognizable backdrop for celebration. The dominant strand came out of the Celtic ritual traditions associated with the festival of Samhain. On this night the seam between the world of the living and the dead was regarded as tenuous and easily penetrated. The dead were said to walk the earth and offerings of food were left out to nourish and placate the wandering souls.

Another strand surfaces in the identification of the foods traditionally associated with the festival of the Roman Goddess Pamona. Worship of Pamona, the goddess of fruits and nuts, becomes the rationale for the use of apples and nuts in connection with Halloween.

The final strand of the holiday is reflected in its name. All Hallows Evening was the night before the great Christian festival of All Saints that celebrated and honored the Christian dead. The name gradually was contracted to today's term, Halloween. The connection between our observance of Halloween and rituals of the festival of All Saints have been difficult to establish. Instead, the name serves to highlight tensions in the activities of the night and beliefs about how things should be.

The weakness in this constructed history of Halloween is that these connections are rather tenuous. Instead, the history of the date justifies both celebration and concerns about the holiday. The result is a ritualized holiday which is highly sensitive to the needs and desires of a particular time and place.

* * * * * *

Halloween, from the end of the nineteenth century through the early years of the twentieth century, was largely celebrated in private homes.[1] Activities for the night were coordinated and led by women who had a wealth of material available to advise them on a proper celebration. Women's magazines, manufacturers' pamphlets and holiday books outlined a night when normal decorum was set aside, and mystery and secrecy were celebrated.[2] Accounts in local newspapers suggest that the guidance was readily and thoroughly incorporated into local celebrations.

This home-based Halloween drew on, and amplified, issues of gender in celebration; in particular, the perception of the home, religious themes, and the boundaries between present, past and future. The rearrangement of physical and mental space is the context in which these issues were presented. Halloween celebrations depended not only on this rearrangement but also critically depended on a twisting of time. The customs of Halloween were routinely presented as relics of "old" or "pagan" customs which had lost their effective power and could therefore be used to enliven and give meaning to leisure time activity. It is the very unreality of Halloween activities, from the early twentieth century perspective, which made them grist for the holiday theme gathering. The poem, "Hallowe'en," written by Robert Burns in 1785, formed the pivot point for interpretation and celebration.[3]

"To Sport that Night": The Structure of Halloween

Miss Jones sat, one early autumn evening, in the family parlor. She was reading the poetry of Bobby Burns. Suddenly she set her book down and declared to her family that, "Halloween celebrations in this day and age are not historically accurate." "We have lost," she asserted, "the real meaning of the holiday." Miss Jones set out to hold an authentic celebration true to "Old England's customs." As reported in a 1907 article in *Harper's Bazaar*, this epitomizes the role Burns' poem, "Hallowe'en," played in shaping the content of Halloween celebrations in this period in the United States.[4]

The poem set the standards for historical veracity or the celebration of a "real" Halloween. The heavy annotation that Burns included on the various matrimonial vaticinations[5] made it a guidebook for the hostess or the writer preparing materials on the mechanics of celebration. In addition, the poem taps the tension surrounding beliefs and superstition. It both warmly embraces the activities and stands back from them as a dispassionate preserver of custom. But, perhaps most critically, the cozy convivial atmosphere of the poem, and its contrast to the forbidding out-of-doors, evoked the identification of the home and its female guide as a place of respite and security.

"Hallowe'en" is also resplendent with festivity and domesticity—and superstition, a positive force in a simple life. The hallowed activities are found round the hearth. It is this vision which makes the poem a touchstone in defining proper celebration in the United States. And so around countless hearths middle-class folks gathered "to sport that night"; reading the future in an effort to return to the simpler and more meaningful celebration portrayed by Burns.

On a night devoted to glimpses at futurity, the dependence on times past as a framework made the future seem more accessible, but still there was an evident need for a guide to interpret past customs and tie them to future possibilities. It is here that the female figure became the embodiment of the night's possibilities. If Burns' poem served to set the ideal Halloween in a convivial evening in the home, then the hostess enlivened the night with her attention to setting and her guidance through these antiquarian, superstitious games. When Miss Jones completes her reading of Burns and transforms the poem into a party, she begins outdoors, her guests gathered around a bonfire, for "none of our efforts to peer into the future can avail until the bad spirits who abound tonight have been consumed."[6]

This twisting of perception between the safe refuge to be found by the hearth and the dangers of the world out of doors is an only slightly intensified representation of the understanding of the home. Throughout the nineteenth century, writers, architects, ministers, and others developed an image of the home as a pivotal social value and the center of a moral life. During this period, the glorification of the home helped to solidify a sense of disjunction between traditional values and the frenzy and chaos associated with city life. Yet, at the same time, the endemic nature of the home was in tension with the ideal that the home also served an educative function, as a place where individuals, particularly children, would learn how to remake society in a better image.[7]

The home, as the institution where moral values were inculcated, became in the nineteenth century the primary institutional focus of religiosity. The home was seen as the place of the family and the family was defined as an institution ordained by God. Old and New Testament examples—of house-holds gathered for worship and worship in homes—were drawn on to legitimate the primacy of home and family in cultural values.

A third way in which domestic religiosity was legitimized was a call on the "mythical power of the peasant past. Writers used Robert Burns' poem 'Cotter's Saturday Night' as a means of tapping into what they conceived of as an ordered meaningful past."[8] This peasant past could be seen in family rituals as well as the ideal design of the home itself. This home was envisioned as set in a rustic, sentimentalized rural setting which evoked an ordered, natural and timeless image. Colleen McDannell notes that:

> Protestant family religion created a sacred time when the change and chaos of the profane world dissolved into the order and meaning of the eternal. The more the family was seen as a refuge in a dangerous world, the more significant domestic rituals became in renewing that sanctuary.[9]

This yearning becomes a feature in home-based entertainment, which forms another level of mediatory activity between the privatized retreat and the nurturing function of the home.

One final feature of the home is important to the ways in which the Halloween party reflected and magnified this image. The guest may have approached the house through its constructed rusticity, but the focus of activity was inside the home itself. A major feature of middle-class homes in this period was the presence of a myriad of private and specialized spaces. Three particular forms of space defined the interior space: "spaces for presenting the home ideal to guests and to the family, space for the production of domestic goods, and spaces for privacy."[10] In particular, the public spaces of the home served a vital communicative role. They helped to present a proper image to guests and family alike.

The restructuring of the home on Halloween night fits within a complex web of structures that the home was understood to demonstrate and preserve. First, recall that the typical guest arrived to find the house darkened. It was inhospitable in presentation and when invited in, the guest was not escorted to the parlor, or other public spaces of the house. Instead guests were entertained in the kitchen, or sometimes the basement—areas that had become the focus of domestic production, and that were generally removed from public view. The setting around the kitchen fire clearly evoked a different era and way of life. The fireplace had become a largely unnecessary aspect of the home, as furnaces and stoves had largely replaced their role in heating the home. Further, to reach the kitchen the guest was escorted through a house profusely decorated to, if not resemble, at least suggest, an out-of-doors or natural setting. Nature could run riot in the home because this display was controlled and created. The distinction between indoors and outdoors was deliberately blurred. And finally the gathering of guests in these spaces of production evoked a different era, the image of a simpler past illustrated in poems like "Hallowe'en" and "Cotter's Saturday Night."

The activities of the night suggest that even in the domestic religiosity which predominated in the period, the need for a productive sense of engagement with one's fate was not being met. The nuts, apples, yarn, dishes, and other domestic objects used in matrimonial and other vaticinations on Halloween are understated. Their focus is on making possible a grasp of the future. In some ways their simplicity hints at the pervasive presence of uncertainty in daily life. If used appropriately, an apple changed from a simple food to an interpretive tool. In the kitchen, it would appear, the celebrants had access to the future. This realm of domestic production was imbued with a curious power on Halloween and other holiday nights.

The Wise Woman: The Female Construction of Celebration

The October 1904 issue of *The Delineator* offered its readers a smorgasbord of "Entertainments for Halloween." The inventive hostess, *The Delineator* reminded, could introduce new ideas that would be appropriately amusing, harmonious and controlled. The reader then was given ideas on autumnal decorations, modern versions of matrimonial games, and games for young children. Or, if the hostess was fatigued with the restless search for a new mode of celebration, she could equally well take the advice tendered by *Harper's Bazaar*: "It is sometimes a relief and a novelty to go back to the oldest of ways."[11]

Articles in women's magazines tended to emphasize the hostess' role in creating a party true to the spirit of the holiday. They are admonished to leave behind their years, dignity, and pessimism when planning for events on this night.[12] The clear implication is that it was up to the hostess to ensure that the atmosphere at the party was appropriate to the traditions of Halloween, even if they represented beliefs no longer held. The hostess, it would appear, was the guiding hand for the celebration.

The notion that the woman of the house would construct an appropriate celebration of Halloween is a logical extension of her role in structuring life inside the home. The structuring of the home as the repository of moral values and education firmly placed the woman of the house in the role of a guide. As Maxine van de Wetering observes, the key symbolic presence in the home was an assumed "settled, ministering 'home angel' inside, the benign and pious and fixed in place mother."[13] This ministering "angel" was responsible not only for ensuring that her home was decorated to evoke this air of religiosity but also for "*guiding* her husband and children, forming their characters through the 'influence' of the home environment."[14] The female spirit who greeted her guests at the door Halloween night and who guided them through a created natural display and the divinatory activities was fulfilling the expected role of the "home angel."

The various permutations on the feminine spirit, from the wise woman, to the witch, to Aunt Chloe, all depended on the role of the woman of the house for their authority in guiding the celebrants through Halloween night. The transformation of the "home angel" into a figure who opened the gates of the future, however, tapped more than the Christian piety of the period and also opened a channel for alternative rituals and religious structures. These focused on the appropriation of superstition in order to celebrate the spirit of the night.

Reading the Future: Superstition and the Hostess as Medium

The appearance of Old Mother Bunch at a Halloween party intimated that a depth of occult information would be forthcoming. The hostess who adopted the Old Mother Bunch role was admonished not to present her as an evil hag, but, rather "as the knowing housewife who in early days had Halloween lore handed down to her through a long line of ancestors."[15]

The hostess' role as a guide through the traditional games

of Halloween implied both a connection with the dimly remembered past and a bold reach into the possible future. Descriptions of Halloween parties suggest that the hostess, often
the only person costumed for the party, might appear as a
ghostly spirit, a witch, a wise woman, a hag, and even occasionally as a mammy.[16]

Her reading of the future, however, existed in tension with
the other basic aspect of Halloween, death. Halloween was a
night when dead spirits wandered the earth. Some of the parlor games described in contemporary magazines could yield a
fortune that implied death within the year. Death was always
a possible outcome of a glimpse into the future world. The
ideal of a female spirit leading games which read the future
and touched on the realm of death evoked some aspects of
Spiritualism. The Halloween parties described in women's
magazines and other sources generally post-date the height of
Spiritualism, but there are some suggestive similarities.

As Ann Braude observed, whether it was honored or ridi-
culed, Spiritualism was ubiquitous at mid-century. The movement met a number of needs in everyday life, including solace
in bereavement, entertainment, a source of livelihood, an alternative to established religious authority, a rebellion against
death and authority, and equality for women. It was a movement in which anyone could participate and check out the evidence for themselves. But most striking for its possible influence on the shaping of Halloween entertainment was the role of
the medium. Braude notes that, by definition, the medium was
usually feminine. The medium evoked the identification of the
female with piety. In addition, Spiritualism, like the late- nineteenth-century Halloween party, was largely home-based.[17]

The advice to Halloween hostesses strikes a remarkably
similar tone. Underneath all of the advice books and articles is
a strong sense of the woman's responsibility for suitable forms
of entertainment that reflect truly the holiday or event celebrated. The hostess is repeatedly admonished to let go of fears
and superstitions and join in the spirit of this festival. Many of
the articles and books provide detailed descriptions and pictures of appropriate charms and tests of the future, relying
heavily on Burns' poem. Finally, the repeated presentation of
the hostess garbed as, and acting as, a wise old female focuses
on the type of authority exercised by the hostess. It is her primary responsibility to *guide* her guests through the proper ac-

tivities and it is she who gives them the materials to interpret their activities. She is an intermediary presenting and interpreting the various future tests, much as the medium in spiritualism carried voices from beyond death.

There is, however, a critical difference between Spiritualism and these parties. Spiritualism was a serious challenge and alternative to Protestantism. Halloween, on the other hand, was an opportunity for entertainment. The possibility that these charms and tests might actually tell the future was roundly denied in the materials available to the hostess. We are, she was reminded, beyond this form of simple superstition; thus while the model of Spiritualism shows some structural parallels to the Halloween party, the parties themselves are, if anything, a firm domestication of the beliefs that drove the movement. So here the leadership of the hostess, the reading of the future, the topsy-turvy house are cast in light-hearted fun—an interesting reflection on the place and role of women both in society in general and in the home.

The domesticated spirit provided, in these parties, an invisible bridge between a complacent present, which relegated anything remotely tinged with superstition to fun and frolic, and the mysterious realm situated somewhere in the past. This faintly ironic interpretation of the holiday was drawn from the meaning read into the seemingly ambivalent sense of superstition which surfaces occasionally in Burns' poem. The poem, as Thompson aptly describes it, juxtaposed the serious relation of a Halloween custom with an ironic outcome. But even in this careful juxtaposition, Burns was unwilling to let go of a supernatural reality; the central stanza of the poem of the dangers of dabbling in this realm:

> . . .sic sportin,
> As seek the *foul Thief* ony place,
>   for him to spae your fortune:
> Nae doubt but ye may get a *sight*
>   Great cause ye hae to fear it;
> For monie a ane has gotten a
>   fright,
> An' liv'd an' di'd deleeret,
>   On sic a night.[18]

This carefully crafted ambiguity toward the supernatural accounts, in large measure, for the role played by the poem in shaping the Halloween celebration in the United States.

This ambivalence is preserved by the women's magazines, local newspaper reporters, and authors of everyday and other holiday works. No one is totally at ease with denigrating the realm of superstition. Perhaps it is because they, like the Grannie of the poem, still find much in the world that is mysterious, unexplained, and often downright dangerous. Perhaps it reflects the lingering association of Halloween with religious ritual.

The Delineator published two particularly striking pieces around this tension in the first twenty years of the twentieth century. The first, by Mary Dawson, who regularly wrote on Halloween for the magazine, was intended to "update and consolidate" Halloween, using both new scientific knowledge and the popular lore associated with the holiday.

Two figures validate the traditional activities of the night. The first is a reiteration of the leadership role given to the feminine spirit who guided the celebration. The Mother Bunch is identified as a "knowing housewife," tapping the role of the woman in the household. Women in the home were both repositories of cultural knowledge and the ones empowered to teach and disseminate it.

Sigmund Freud is the second figure used by Dawson. Her article, "Dreams Make Fun for Halloween," heralds Freud's research as having stamped the "jumbled visions of our pillows (with) new importance." Peering into the future through dreams, and, by implication, the other divinatory activities of the night, was therefore a valid and useful activity. Dawson here engages in the desire to explain and validate the activities of the night in terms acceptable to the modern world—terms that will sever the activities from the strictly superstitious or frolicsome realm.[19]

The other article appeared five years later and moved this transition even farther along the superstition-science continuum. "Halloween Occult and Shuddery" seeks to demonstrate how far we have come from "our grandmothers." In the world of the 1920s, science is proclaimed to have triumphed over superstition, and therefore the appropriate venue for the Halloween celebration is the formal seance. Edna Erle Wilson notes that:

> for countless generations young men and maidens have thrilled
> to the Halloween fortunes revealed to them by apple peelings

and magic gipsy (sic) brews, but an *entirely new method* is introduced in soliciting aid *via the ouija-board*.[20]

Wilson concluded that the traditional symbols of the holiday had been outgrown and that in their place was a whole new array of symbols. The implication is that activities of the night were on the right track, but that the "grandmothers" lacked the proper tools to truly divine the future. Wilson seems to suggest that it is not the probing of the future or the communication with the dead that is superstitious, but rather the methods employed.

Halloween, then, was a celebration which allowed for the atypical to be expressed and enjoyed. Its gentle twisting of time, space, and gender roles suggests some recognition of differing perspectives. But the twisting is so subtle and directed at leisure that it strongly highlights the increasingly subservient role of religious beliefs—and of women—in the culture.

Halloween is a night to play with superstition. But never is there a real hint of the dark side to death, the past or the future. These are realms that remain ultimately out of the feminine spirit's reach, for on the day after, order returns and her role as spiritual and cultural guide recedes once again into the gentle background of the home.

This is particularly obvious when Halloween celebrations move outdoors and become activities for children. While many of the symbols and ideas are drawn from these home-based parties, the men are fully in control of the new celebrations, which highlight and preserve the values of democratic citizenship. With the advent of outdoor festivities, the tenuous link between worlds and possibilities was rudely severed, and the generative and structuring role played by feminine spirits faded from memory.

Notes

1. There were also parties held in churches and some schools but they followed the same basic structure. In particular, they were for fairly small, intimate groups.

2. Articles in women's magazines included educational information about the holiday, sample menus, decorating advice and suggested thematic approaches. For a sample see Lina Beard, "Witchery Games of Halloween," *The Delineator* (October 1904): 576-579; Jane Calhoun, "A Hallowe'en Supper," *Harper's Bazaar* (November 1910):

641; Mary Dawson, "A Tam O'Shanter Hallowe'en Party," *The Delineator* (October 1914): 26, "Fun for Hallowe'en," *Ladies Home Journal* (October 1907): 78; Helen Kenney, "Hallowe'en Favors," *Harper's Bazaar* (November 1911): 516. Manufacturer's pamphlets provided similar information but with an emphasis on the use of their products in proper celebration. The best example of these is *Dennison's Bogie Book: 11th Annual Edition* (Framingham, MA: Dennison Manufacturing Company, 1913). Dennison produced paper goods of all kinds for home use. Finally, there were numerous books on holiday celebration, both those specific to Halloween and more general treatments of holidays. See, for example, *The Book of Hallowe'en* (Boston: Lothrop, Lee and Shepard Co., 1919); Martha Russell Orne, *Hallowe'en: How to Celebrate it with Appropriate Games and Ceremonies* (New York: Fitzgerald Publishing Corporation, 1898); Elizabeth F. Guptill, Laura Rountree Smith, and others, *Bright Ideas for Hallowe'en* (Lebanon, Ohio: March Brothers, 1920); Marie Irish, *Hallowe'en Hilarity* (Dayton: Paine Publishing Company, 1924); Mary E. Blain, *Games for Hallowe'en* (New York: Barse and Hopkins, 1912); Lettie C. Van Derveer, *Halloween Happenings* (Boston: Walter H. Barker Co., 1921).

3. Robert Burns, *The Poems and Songs of Robert Burns*, ed. James Kinsley, 3 volumes (Oxford: Clarendon, 1968), vol. 1, 152-163.

4. Bertha Hasbrook, "A Nutcrack Night Party," *Harper's Bazaar* (November 1907): 1106-1109.

5. The term vaticination means a prediction of an inspired nature. It was the term used in many of the magazines to describe the games.

6. Hasbrook, "Nutcrack Night" 1106.

7. Clifford E. Clark, "Domestic Architecture as an Index to Social History: The Romantic Revival and the Cult of Domesticity in America, 1840-1870," *Journal of Interdisciplinary History* 7/1 (Summer 1976): 33-56; Maxine van de Wetering, "The Popular Concept of 'Home' in Nineteenth Century America," *Journal of American Studies* 18 (1984): 5-28; Gwendolyn Wright, *Moralism and the Model Home: Domestic Architecture and Cultural Conflict in Chicago, 1873-1913* (Chicago: University of Chicago Press, 1980); Jan Cohn, *The Palace or the Poorhouse: The American Home as a Cultural Symbol* (East Lansing: Michigan State University Press, 1979); Kirk Jeffrey, "The Family as Utopian Retreat for the City: The Nineteenth Century Contribution," *Soundings* 55 (1972): 21-41; Colleen McDannell, *The Christian Home in Victorian America, 1840-1900* (Bloomington: Indiana University Press, 1986).

8. McDannell, *Christian Home* 78.

9. McDannell, *Christian Home* 104.

10. Wright, *Moralism and the Model Home* 33-34.

11. Ruth Virginia Sackett, Mary Dawson, and Grace B. Ward, "En-

tertainments for Halloween: An Autumn-Leaf Jollification, A Goose Party, and Guessing Cities," *The Delineator* (October 1904): 638-640; "Quaint Hallowe'en Customs" 578.

12. Calhoun, "A Hallowe'en Supper" 641.

13. van de Wetering, "Popular Concept of the 'Home'" 13.

14. Wright, *Moralism and the Model Home* 10

15. Mary Dawson, "Dreams Make Fun for Halloween," *The Delineator* (October 1915): 21.

16. Edna Erle Wilson, "The Dixie Dance for All-Hallow Eve," *The Delineator* (October 1919): 96; Calhoun, "A Hallowe'en Supper"; Dawson, "Tam O'Shanter"; Dawson, "Dreams Make Fun."

17. Ann Braude, *Radical Spirits: Spiritualism and Women's Rights in Nineteenth Century America* (Boston: Beacon Press, 1989); and Howard Kerr, *Mediums, and Spirit-Rappers, and Roaring Radicals* (Urbana: University of Illinois Press, 1972).

18. Burns, *Poems* 157-158.

19. Dawson, "Dreams Make Fun" 21.

20. Edna Erle Wilson, "Hallowe'en, Occult and Shuddery," *The Delineator* (October 1920): 65-66 [emphasis added].

4

Trespassing the Boundaries: A Reflection on Men, Women, and Jewish Space

Barbara Borts

> When you came into the House [of Parliament], I felt as though
> a woman had entered my bathroom and I had nothing to pro-
> tect me except my sponge."
> —Winston Churchill to Nancy Astor, first woman MP,
> at her first session of Parliament[1]

AT THE TIME OF THE WRITING OF THIS ARTICLE, A DREADFUL HOLO-
caust is occurring in the former country of Yugoslavia, as one
nation attempts to "cleanse" its territory of another, "alien"
nation. However, had this article been written at any other
point in time, one would have been able to point to another
war, another population expulsion, another vicious confrontation about territory.

Territorialism is a well-documented phenomenon. Animals—humans, as well others—stake out their patches
through urinating, through fighting, through expulsion,
through terror. This reflects deep-rooted needs to belong, to
have definable spaces of intimacy and comfortableness, to be
among others who will constitute one's community and one's
people, to define oneself through space and in a place. Such

needs, universal as they are, do have legitimacy, despite attempts to criticize them away. "Imagine there's no boundaries . . . nothing to kill or die for . . ." The need to delineate one's territory is, at its best, the need to set up Home, a palace, a refuge from strangeness, a place to belong. Unfortunately, at its worst, it is about power and exclusion, about hierarchies of quality, and the violence people will use to defend those boundaries.

Abraham Joshua Heschel, one of the most sublime of Jewish thinkers, taught that Judaism is a religion of "holiness-in-time" instead of holiness-in-space. He wrote that in Christianity, the palace of space is the sacred object—a church, a cathedral, a sanctuary. He wanted us to be wary of sacralising space, of making a god out of a territory instead of letting God in every and anywhere. Shabbat, Heschel's purest moment of holiness-in-time, is to be celebrated as a twenty-five hour sanctuary carved of mundanity exalted at home, in bed, in a park, with friends and family—and with the community, in a synagogue. It begins with the lighting of candles, not with stepping over the threshold of a particular building.[2]

And yet Heschel would himself davven (pray traditionally) in synagogues where the use of space was perhaps debased—that is, synagogues that carved out separate territory for men and for women.

Many rationales in Jewish tradition explain the curtain of demarcation, the mechitzah, drawn between men and women at prayer in an Orthodox synagogue: women distract men; women are not obligated in communal prayer; women are enjoined to cultivate the private, personal sides of spirituality. And in response, many women infuse the separate space with their own meaning: it breaks up the family assumptions of non-Orthodox Jewish prayer, in which people come and sit in family groups, possibly alienating those not in a family; it offers women tranquility and independence from men; it allows women to find a voice that might otherwise be drowned out; it permits women time in the company of other women. In this vein, many women who were not raised Orthodox and who would consider themselves feminist have, nonetheless, chosen to davven in an Orthodox environment where the kavvanah (intent and purpose) is passionate and the ruach (the spirit) is intense, and to derive great satisfaction from their prayer.[3]

It is certainly legitimate for groups to at times isolate themselves from others and to claim meaning in that separation. Jews need time to pray and play with other Jews; blacks together explore their strength and history; women experiment, find their voices, and support each other; men talk and forge new ways of becoming men, friends, and companions. To borrow from Erich Fromm, sometimes groups need freedom, not from, but to—not as escape and exclusion, but rather as an acknowledgement that all human beings need to find their roots and their place, to be nurtured by their families and intimate communities, to learn from this how to build something solid to bring back to the world. One might even say that such boundaries serve the needs of Heschel's Shabbat, creating sanctuaries in time for refreshment and renewal.

This is, however, patently not the purpose of separation in the synagogues of Judaism, nor in the ritual life of the Jewish people. When there exists only one institution—namely, the synagogue—and one group claims control of it, then this is nothing more than exclusion, and as such, it violates the principle of "freedom to." If women make the best of it when they choose to remain within the Orthodox world, then they are doing just that—redefining and reinterpreting the imposed conditions to give themselves control over it.[4]

Some enlightened Orthodox women, with supportive and daring rabbis, have also begun to make much more creative use of separation altogether, by forming women's 'minyanim' (enclosed in quotes because they still do not count themselves a true minyan), a community of ten obligated in prayer, which can thus omit those prayers which tradition says may only be said in the presence of ten or more men.[5]

Were women who accepted the principles of the separation of the sexes at prayer allowed to design a mechitzah, it would be literally that—a divider between equal parts of the room, with equal access to the bima, the Torah, and the obligations of communal worship. Such a division, even if not to everyone's taste, could be supported because it was chosen (not imposed), because it was mutual, and because it served to create sacred time within the confines of sacred—not exclusive and excluding—space.

Why spend time on these issues if one is a woman rabbi in the Reform movement? We in the non-Orthodox world assume that these are not our issues, that we have evolved in our understanding of the nature of space and can now deal with more profound issues about the nature of prayer and God language. But I believe that this may not be the case. For thousands of years, men have excluded women from major spaces of life in much the same way and with much the same violence as they have fought other men who have encroached upon their territories and trespassed upon their boundaries; this has a demonstrable effect in the wider world. Surely the same must be the case in the Jewish world, where centuries of male ritual and religious domination must leave its imprint in the collective Jewish memory.[6]

Concerns about preserving all-male ritual space are certainly not limited to religious space. As the opening quote for this article indicates, Parliament, the birthplace of democracy, was for some reduced to a gentlemen's privy violated by women upon its first integration. In another instance some years ago, again in England, a woman breast-feeding a baby in a pub was asked to leave, and then banned. The complaints from the men included the plaintive observation that the pub was really a space (with the boys) away from home, which should not resemble home (and thus, mixed territory of women and men) with babies and knitting. As an interesting parallel, I remember that when I first went to discuss the possibility of becoming one of England's first female rabbis, one male rabbi was delighted at the thought of more women at meetings comfortingly clicking knitting needles in the midst of the fracas of male battle. On the one hand, women in male space—even liberal male space—are to be silent and unnoticed as women; on the other, women in male space are to be obviously, flagrantly, and stereotypically female, so as to avoid there being any confusion of gender or purpose.

One could list many other territories that are free of women—professional clubs, organizations, committees, political arenas, and so on, in which women are under-represented or not present at all. Not all areas must always be mixed, but when the place in question is the religious center, professional body, or government, it is startling to see no women there. One is simply astonished that women, virtually half of the population, are still deemed pariahs in some places, invisible in others—that "their place is not the world."

When women do succeed in trespassing on men's space, they are often punished for it. Rape is apparently a real and present terror even at our most prestigious universities, some of which have only comparatively recently admitted women to study. Sexual harassment and discrimination is endemic in many fields, including among the clergy, a rather classic professional example of women "violating" a heretofore male-only preserve. In one very progressive and admirable rabbinical college, hailed as a leader in the movement for women in Jewish life, women who teach and study there still feel excluded and ignored, and there is a constant battle to add a feminist analysis to existing courses, not as special "Women in/ and_____" offerings. One Sunday afternoon in 1991, women students and faculty members got together to imagine a rabbinical college guided by and really true to a feminist vision. Such unease, such sense of trespass, in the very heartland of progressive Judaism! There is a lesson here. These and other anecdotes drawn from pioneering women's experiences remind us that, when we progressives believe that the major battles of tradition have been won and we are ready for bigger and better things, we are deluded.

It is not surprising that primitive attachments to space and its concomitant power still drive the Jewish world. The Jewish theologian Richard Rubenstein once wrote that the most archaic aspects of religion are the ones with the most potency, and that the rational exhortations of rabbis and preachers will never move us in the way that the old biblical cult moved our ancestors.[7] The force of ancestral memory, of old rites and strongly held conviction, cannot easily be shaken, not through the pulpit nor even the article.

Interestingly, Judaism has enshrined the division of male and female worlds in halacha, Jewish law, reinforcing male territoriality through posited divine injunction and daily practice. By tradition, there are 613 commandments derived from the Torah, the five books of Moses. These inviolable ur-halachot are divided into positive (you shalls) and negative (you shall nots) precepts. Of these we are taught that while women are obligated in all of the negative commandments, they [we] are *exempt* from time-bound positive ones—that is, any that need to be fulfilled within a specified time. The list of women's exemptions includes attending morning prayer (although women are supposed to pray by themselves); wearing the tallit and tefillin (prayer shawl and phylacteries, adjuncts to prayer); dwelling in the Sukkah (Tabernacle) during the festival of Sukkot; and even learning Talmud.[8]

The usual explanation of this *exemption* (and the word is italicized to emphasize the courteous nature of the initial phrasing) is that women are enjoined to cultivate the private, inward side of their nature, to remain individuals, and to assume primary responsibility for the home and for child-rearing, even if they pursue an outside career. To obligate women who are private and self-contained and who are busy with the ceaseless demands of domesticity by adding the burden of appearing at certain places at certain times, would be a cruelty—thus, exemption.[9]

However—and this is a big however—there are inconsistencies in this argument. There are, for example, many time-bound positive commandments that are incumbent upon women—for instance, lighting Shabbat candles not less than eighteen minutes before the onset of the Sabbath, a commandment which is one of women's gravest responsibilities. Women are also obligated to hear the shofar (ram's horn), which is blown during certain parts of the obligatory New Year service. And so on. It is not that the early rabbis themselves were unaware of the contradictions; indeed, they list some time-bound positive commandments to which women *are* obligated, and some that are not time-bound but from which women are also exempt, then conclude that, nonetheless, the discrepancies do not disprove the general rule.[10]

When one examines the texts carefully, one notes that almost all of the mitzvot from which women are "exempt" have to do with *space*, not time. Such an understanding encompasses virtually all of the exemptions, from communal prayer and study and dwelling in the sukkah, as well as the obligations, from Shabbat candle lighting to attending a seder during the festival of Passover. The former occur in the synagogue or places in which men congregate to learn and discuss; the latter occur in the home, the rightful place for women.[11]

This observation is bolstered by some further burdens upon Jewish women. We are told that women's separation from men in synagogue derives not just from the fact that women's presence is optional at prayer, but also from the fact that women are temptresses, whether wittingly or unwittingly, liable to distract men from the serious nature of the divine-human encounter.[12] Even in the spaces in which women are allowed to appear—the home, the street, the concert hall—women are to behave as if they are invisible. Orthodox Jewish women are taught to dress modestly; some groups require women to cover their hair; woman's voice in song is to be silent. The latter prohibition led recently to a rather ridiculous exchange in the Anglo-Jewish press about the advisability of male attendance at the opera!

In the case of the modern desire of progressive women to wear a tallit or prayer shawl, one needs to examine the halachic evidence, even for men and women who are otherwise non-halachic. Texts about that are also intriguing. Although the authoritative code of Jewish law, the Shulchan Arukh, states that women are to wear fringes on the corners of four-cornered garments, a later gloss adds that if a woman were to do so, she would appear to be showing off, being immodest. To this day, few women wear a tallit or kippah at prayer, and very few have experimented with alternatives. One gets the impression when one enters a Reform or Conservative synagogue that the community of identifiable Jews is still male, hence the distaste, unease, even fear and loathing which some men (and women) express about those women who are noticeable, who do mark themselves off, as *Jewish*, through wearing ritual prayer garments. Especially in a place where the men and women sit together, there apparently still needs to be a way for men to claim their own space. Articles still discuss the Jew and his wife, in much the same way as a farmer will also be accompanied in a newspaper caption by his wife. As with the woman breast-feeding in the pub, apparently the threat of devouring femaleness necessitates women's silent and surreptitious habitation of public territory. Women should neither be seen nor heard—and the parallel with the original statement about children is chillingly apt.

Using this understanding to review the material of Jewish law, Jewish male and female resistance to change becomes clearer. The thrust of four thousand years of Jewish history has been to exclude women from all ritual places but the home, essentially creating out of Jewish observance all of the characteristics of a men's club—and some of the locker room behavior that accompanies such gatherings. One has only to look at the palpable hatred and rage on the faces of the men who gathered against the Women at the Wall[13] to understand what it is that men and women need to uncover. And this does not appertain solely to the Jewish world. In fact, there are men who so dislike the thought of women existing in the same space with them—namely, the world—that fear of rape, assault and murder keeps most women "in their place" and unfree to claim all spaces.

Further insights into this require the service of an anthropsychologist, but it is perhaps not too difficult to understand the way in which this compels us by searching our own lives for paradigms. I know that I can feel intruded upon in my office if, when I enter, I see someone in there using it as if it were their own, or if guests come to stay who then make themselves too much at home.

Sometimes insecurity about essential inner identity can necessitate finding identity outside oneself; as the male has tended to identify maleness with sexual conquest and other uses of the male external organ, space becomes another external source of identity. One suspects that a part of the desire of successful business executives to get larger offices, to move into grand houses, and to purchase large luxury cars derives from and in turn supports this need: those with the most territory are the most worthwhile. In Jewish tradition, despite the fact that the rabbis are at pains to describe the work of women as equal in value to that of men, the texts are nonetheless replete with paeans of praise about study and [public] prayer. A "good" Jew is one who performs these mitzvot; hence, no woman can really be a "good" Jew. Her work will always be secondary, if value does indeed rest upon study and prayer.[14]

Exclusive space is unambiguous and demands no negotiation of role and function, much as traditional marriage assumed certain divisions of labor into which people could fall without analysis or anxiety. Women's place was the kitchen, men's the garage; women were upstairs quilting, men outside mending fishing nets, and so on. You knew who you were by what you weren't—and this may be particularly acute for men, whose masculine identity is seemingly so frail. To go into a shul as a man meant that you were the Jew, you were special, privileged, chosen. It did not even matter so much what you knew or could do—you were a man and therefore were entitled to sit nearer the torah, touch it, don a tallis. To this day lay women will often refuse to wear a tallit, saying that this is for female rabbis who are Jewishly knowledgeable, ignoring the fact that there are no criteria for the male to wear one, no examinations to test a man's worthiness.

All this has been and is in the process of being overturned. It is an unsettling, anxious world, the one feminists wish to build upon existing progressive structures. To no longer have space (and thus, power) simply by virtue of masculinity, bolstered by the physical exclusion of the opposite, threatening sex, might mean that one may not get a job, or mitzvah—an honor during the service. It questions the assumption that being male entitles one, and threatens the male meritocracy. It means sharing, rethinking, finding new sources of identity.

Sharing space—whether in the synagogue, the office, or the world—equally between men and women is the real and most fundamental battle. Some years ago, eminent Jewish theologians Cynthia Ozick and Judith Plaskow debated the right arena in which to push for change in the Jewish world. Ozick maintained that the "question" was sociological and the solution was to enlarge on the numbers of women in Jewish life. Plaskow countered that the right question was theological and that until the language we used was free of gender-specific and oppressively male imagery, there would be no progress.[15]

Many Jewish women have propounded first one solution, then the other, and of course, both types of change are vital, Ozick's particularly so in the light of the thesis of this article. But no amount of modification in the liturgy, nor increased presence of women in the synagogue and on the bima, will allay the underlying angst. Men will, as is beginning to happen, simply opt out of Jewish life in the non-Orthodox Jewish world.

The synagogue, the house of study, the streets and parks of our towns, are not male territory and women are not trespassers on a masculine preserve. This point needs to be made over and over again, in all the ways available to us, through the presence of females in roles of prominence and in the sacred texts, and through real work on the authentic humanness of woman (and man). If we could find ways to tackle this enduring sense of ownership and trespass, a challenging and painful prospect, we may also encounter the only way which can offer people opportunity, safety, freedom to be. It seems that the issue has real significance beyond the world of Jewish observance.

Heschel wrote: "To gain control of the world of space is certainly one of our tasks. The danger begins when in gaining power in the realms of space, we forfeit all aspirations in the realm of time. There is a realm of time where the goal is not to have, but to be, not to win, but to share, not to subdue, but to be in accord."[16] To return for a last moment to the Jewish world: we are in a crisis of belief and commitment, and we need to concentrate our energies on the transcendent side of our task. The synagogue should not be a battleground—it is, rather, to be a place of essential existence, of harmony, and of contentment, a world without boundaries between man and woman, the world and the Jew, humans and God. What a radical and liberating concept that is.

Notes

1. Louisa Saunders, in *The Guardian* (10 October 1989).

2. Abraham Joshua Heschel, *The Sabbath* (New York: Farrar, Straus, and Giroux, 1951).

3. See, for example, Susan Weidman Schneider, *Jewish and Female* (New York: Simon and Schuster, 1984) chapter 2. There has also been interesting research into women who are "Ba'alat Teshuvah," denoting those assuming a traditional Jewish life.

4. The issue of feminism and the Orthodox world is interesting. On the one hand, it would seem that the expression "Orthodox feminist" is an oxymoron; however, liberal Jewish feminists have been admonished not to dismiss women from the traditional Jewish world simply because their choices do not seem to fit liberal expectations about religion and the women's movement. Many Orthodox and Chassidic women are highly educated and work in responsible positions, and nonetheless accept the system of role separation set them by tradition, at least to some extent or another. For more on this see Blu Greenberg, *On Women and Judaism* (Philadelphia: The Jewish Publication Society, 1981).

5. Schneider, *Jewish and Female* 67-68.

6. And, it must be noted, great numbers of otherwise liberal and even secular, unobservant Jews believe that real Jewish authenticity lies in the ultra-Orthodox world. The Lubavitch Chassidim, for instance, receive many donations from such Jews who believe that

they are the ones ensuring the survival of Judaism. See, for example, Leonard Fein, *Where Are We?* (New York: Harper and Row, 1988) 45-46.

7. Richard L. Rubenstein, *After Auschwitz* (Indianapolis: Bobbs-Merrill, 1966) 92.

8. Talmud Bavli - Kiddushin 33b

9. David ben Joseph Abudarham (14th century), *Sefer Abudurham*: III; Moshe Meiselman, *Jewish Women in Jewish Law* (New York: KTAV, 1978).

10. Talmud Bavli, Kiddushin 33b - 34a.

11. There is at least one discrepancy in my theory, to be fair, and that relates to the obligation of women to hear the Torah reading. The Torah would be read during a morning service on the Sabbath, Festivals, Mondays and Thursdays, and on Shabbat afternoon. However, one could imagine that the holiest of texts must be heard even by those otherwise silenced in the congregation. In a similar manner, many Jewish women believe that, just as they may not touch a man during the period of their "niddah" (menstrual ritual impurity), so [how much the more so!, to quote a principle of Jewish interpretation] must they not touch the Torah. This is a misconception—the holiness of the Torah cannot be affected by ritual impurity. (Shulchan Arukh, "Orach Chayyim" 84:1).

12. Meiselman, *Jewish Women* 142-143.

13. The Women at the Wall is a coalition of Jewish women of all denominations who gather regularly to pray at the Western [Wailing] Wall in Jerusalem, wearing tallitot (prayer shawls) and reading from the Torah. Needless to say, this arouses the ire of the ultra-Orthodox keepers of the wall.

14. Pirkei Avot 1:2. The third in that trio of supporting structures is "deeds of loving kindness" which are obligatory on both women and men.

15. Cynthia Ozick, "Notes toward Finding the Right Question" and Judith Plaskow, "The Right Question is Theological" in *On Being a Jewish Feminist*, ed. Susannah Heschel (New York: Schocken Books, 1983) 120ff; 223ff.

16. Heschel, *The Sabbath* 3.

5

Empowering Spirits: Women and *Zaar* Spirit Possession

Sheila Webster Boneham

WOMEN IN TRADITIONAL MUSLIM SOCIETIES ACQUIRE AND EXERT power in many ways. One is *zaar*[1] spirit possession, a folk illness found in Egypt and Sudan,[2] particularly in Nubia, the region that straddles the two nations from the Libyan border to the shores of the Suez Canal. Originally *zaar* was found only in villages, among the lower class. Now, *zaar* is found in Cairo, and includes women from the middle and upper classes, though the majority are still of peasant stock.

Although the details of *zaar* possession vary from group to group, village to village, the spirits, the symptoms of possession, and the rituals used to appease the spirits are characteristically similar enough to be lumped together and used for drawing certain general interpretive conclusions. My intent here is not to give a specific ethnographic description of any one incident of *zaar* possession, instead to describe the characteristics of possession and to show how women use the belief system and rituals not only for catharsis[3] but also to achieve some measure of power beyond that which they normally hold.

The Meaning of "Power"

"Power" here means the ability to effect change or stasis through methods both overt and covert. "Authority" is power with the force of society behind it, that is, socially sanctioned power. But the concept of power is problematic, particularly when dealing with traditional societies where everyone, male and female, is limited by social and cultural conventions. Women in traditional societies, including traditional Muslim societies, are often seen by westerners as downtrodden and powerless. The return of the veil in many parts of the Islamic[4] world has encouraged that view, but field studies reveal a more complicated picture of women's status.

Before the 1970s, the bulk of our knowledge of non-western cultures was based on the work of male ethnographers whose only access to the distaff side of the traditionally gender-segregated societies in which they worked was through the men. Although a sizeable body of research was produced by trained scholars, much was also the work of missionaries, soldiers, adventurers, and others with varying degrees of cultural sensitivity, language facility, and honesty, especially in the late nineteenth and early twentieth centuries. Some had particular axes to grind, and most were influenced by Victorian notions of cultural darwinism, which held that English elite society was the epitome of human development toward which all other societies were struggling, with varying degrees of success. And of course, in that ultimate society (as in all others), women were held to be naturally inferior to men. Even those men who strove to present cultural data as completely and accurately as possible were stifled by the economics and etiquette of publishing, and more than one manuscript was "cleaned up" before publication by an editor. Even under the best circumstances, the data collected and published about Muslim women was heavily filtered.

It is doubtful that men really know what goes on among women (or vice versa) in any society. In societies where women are off-limits to all but a small circle of men under a limited set of circumstances, we can be certain that men know only what the women want them to know.[5] What male ethnographers have to work with in such situations is whatever is left after the women decide what to tell their men, and those men decide what to tell the ethnographer, and the words are translated with varying measures of accuracy of both denotation and connotation. Very often what is left is not much, and is distorted. It is a game of "telephone"[6] with cultural, linguistic, and gender twists.[7]

In the past two decades the ethnographic literature on Muslim women has benefitted dramatically from the work of trained female ethnographers, both native and non-native to the cultures they have studied. One result of their work has been a re-evaluation of the concept of "power" and of the dynamics of gender relations in Muslim societies.

The Nature of the Zaar

Zaar spirits are a form of *jinn* (singular *jinni*), or what in English we commonly call "genies." The *jinn*, like human beings, are divided into different races and sexes. They inhabit a sort of invisible "parallel universe," although from time to time they make contact with people. Angels also inhabit the earth, but people seem to be less likely to be in contact with them than with demons. The *jinn* are referred to in the Quran and are therefore part of orthodox Islam, as well as of various folk belief systems throughout the Middle East.[8] Orthodox Islam does not support *zaar* ceremonies, which involve a number of forbidden activities, such as communication with evil spirits, unsanctioned animal sacrifice, and the use of intoxicants. But opposition to the ceremonies is usually mild, because some Quranic passages are interpreted as linking the *jinn* to illness.[9]

The symptoms that Nubians interpret as *zaar*-induced would in western terms be classed primarily as various forms of anxiety reactions, hysteria, and depression, although more severe problems like schizophrenia are sometimes treated as *zaar* possession. Persons suffering from such neuroses are not regarded as abnormal, however; in view of the pressures of living in Nubian society, that seems a reasonable assessment.

Behaviors characteristically associated with acute possession include dissociation, paralysis, apathy, withdrawal, loss of appetite, refusal to work, insomnia, and a desire to die. In addition, the victim may complain of unlocalized pain and may suffer "an unaccountable wasting away and progressive weakening, accompanied by listlessness and loss of appetite."[10] The victim might be said to suffer a chronic, low-grade sort of disease of spirit with occasional acute flare-ups. Indeed, it is the lack of ease in her own spirit that makes a woman a prime candidate for *zaar* illness.

It is only when other treatments have failed and symptoms of *zaar* possession have become acute that steps are taken to treat the victim through a *zaar* ceremony. Possession by a *zaar* spirit is considered to be a permanent condition, and the purpose of the *zaar* ritual is not to exorcise the possessing spirit but to appease it. The person may marry her *zaar*[11] and in many cases she takes on a continuing responsibility to hold a *zaar* ceremony once a year and to attend other people's ceremonies.

The Zaar Ritual

Zaar ritual activities commence when a patient fails to respond to treatment by traditional healers who try various folk remedies (for instance, herbal medicines, physical manipulation, or blood-letting) and sometimes by western-trained doctors. The "sheikh of the *zaar*," or *zaar* healer, makes a diagnosis of the patient's illness. If the source of the problem is found to be a *zaar* spirit, the *zaar* healer recommends that a *zaar* ceremony be held. The optimum ceremony runs from morning until night for seven days, but a quick recovery, mild illness, or lack of ability to pay may foreshorten the event to anywhere from one to three days.

Men often play major roles as leaders and musicians, but *zaar* ceremonies are held primarily by and for women. Usually held in someone's house, the ceremony requires a room large enough to accommodate thirty to a hundred or more women while leaving an open area for the dancers. Some members of the audience are initiates, women who consider themselves to have overcome *zaar* illness and who are obligated to attend such ceremonies to placate their spirits. (Though not the conventional anthropological usage, I would emphasize the ambiguity of "spirit" here, since the possessing spirit, the *zaar*, comes to the woman whose inner spirit, her soul, has somehow gone—or been pushed—astray.) The others in the audience are there to support their friends and relatives, or for entertainment.

The physical setting of a *zaar* ceremony assaults the senses. The doors and windows are kept closed and the lights are kept low. The room is hot and fragrant with incense, perfume, and sweat. Once the ceremony is underway, the *zaar* healer uses very loud drumming to summon the spirits, each of which responds to its own rhythm. Members of the audience wear new or clean clothing to please the inhabiting spirits, adding to the "specialness" of the event. Sensory overload contributes to altered states of consciousness, helping to induce trances in the focal patient, members of the audience, and the healer.

The patient being treated becomes a "bride" for the ceremony. She is usually clothed in a white dress and white veil, adorned with as much gold jewelry as possible, and perfumed. The rims of her eyes are painted black with *kohl*, a heavy black eyeliner. Her palms, soles, and legs are stained reddish-brown with henna. She sits unmoving before the audience like a bride at her wedding. She is the center of attention.

The details of the *zaar* ritual vary with the severity of the illness, the local customs, and the practices of the individual healer. For instance, if the illness is severe, the healer may perform purification rituals before beginning the singing and dancing of the *zaar* ritual proper. Smoke from incense is commonly passed over and around the patient for ritual cleansing.

Music and dancing are always part of a *zaar* ritual, and the healer must be an accomplished drummer knowledgeable about the songs and rhythms used to summon individual *zaar* spirits. Various types of tambourines, including the *tar* and *dabella*, are used, as is a *tisht*, or metal washtub, and drums. While in their various trances, the possessed women dance, and the dances are frequently erotic, the movements clearly suggestive of copulation.

The healer plays a number of songs, each addressed to a different spirit. Kennedy describes the results:

> When a spirit associated with some person in the audience is called, that person begins to shake in her seat, then makes her way to the central dancing area, sometimes dancing and trembling till she falls exhausted to the floor.[12]

Sometimes several members of the audience will respond to the same rhythm, indicating that a class of spirit rather than an individual *zaar* spirit is involved.

Before agreeing to leave, the spirit or spirits usually make demands for specific items such as jewelry, new clothing, or expensive foods. Since the spirit has no physical form, it speaks through the patient. Kennedy reports, however, that sometimes the demands are rather outlandish, "such as orders to wear a green veil or dunk one's head in a pail of water."[13] And not infrequently, the demands are for things forbidden to women, such as cigarettes. The spirit may also become verbally abusive to or about certain people. Through the medium of the possessed woman, the spirit may, for instance, call the woman's husband names or curse and berate him for any of a multitude of sins from abusiveness to stinginess to impotence. The spirit may also ask that the husband (or someone else) purchase certain things for the woman—new clothing, jewelry, housewares. Such public outcries from a wife are not normally permitted, but since the spirit, not the wife, is responsible, and since the *jinn* are part of orthodox belief, the husband usually complies with the spirit's demands when they are presented to him. It should be noted, though, that despite social pressures encouraging belief in the *zaar* and in the need for and efficacy of the *zaar* rituals, on occasion the costs of a case exceed the husband's willingness to pay. At least one expensive case of Egyptian *zaar* possession has "been cured by a beating."[14]

The friends and relatives of the possessed woman are required to take care of her while she is in the trance, and to pacify the spirit. The healer will bring the woman back to consciousness after a few minutes by singing a special song.

During the course of the ceremony the healer may also become possessed, often by a series of different spirits each requiring a change of costume, personality, accent, and even dialect. Fortune-telling and folk healing of non-*zaar* ailments commonly occur among members of the audience during *zaar* ceremonies.

The *zaar* ceremony ends with an animal sacrifice. As does the length of the ceremony itself, the type of animal sacrificed depends on the wishes and wealth of the sponsoring patient or her family as well as on the patient's condition. Routine annual *zaar* ceremonies and those of sponsors of limited means may offer a cock or a pair of pigeons, while a full seven-day ceremony will likely involve the sacrifice of several chickens on the first, third, and fifth days and a lamb or sheep on the seventh.

Typically a black or white cock (the color determined by the healer when the initial diagnosis was made) is killed over the patient on the third day, and her face, hands, and legs are smeared with the animal's blood. The next evening the bird is cooked and then eaten by the healer and patient.

> On the seventh day, the patient ceremonially straddles the lamb or sheep holding the slaughtering knife in her hand. After five piasters have been placed in the animal's mouth, its throat is cut by the sheikh. The ritual is continued by wrapping the five piasters that were in the animal's mouth in a piece of cloth and tying it to the patient's right hand. The hot blood of the sacrificial animal is rubbed all over the body and face, and some of it is mixed in a potion with cloves, henna and water. After drinking this potion, the sick person ritually steps across the dead animal seven times.[15]

At the end of the final sacrifice, the *zaar* spirit is usually considered to be pacified. *Fatta*, a traditional Nubian ceremonial food, is prepared with meat of the sacrificial animal and is eaten by the patient and her guests who are possessed by *zaar* spirits. Those who have not been possessed do not eat the *fatta* for fear that they will become possessed, and all remains of the animal after the meal must be collected and tossed into the Nile River so that unsuspecting animals will not eat it and be contaminated. Finally, the patient and those guests who have been possessed bathe their faces and legs in the Nile. In some cases the patient is advised to remain in seclusion for forty days, as new brides do.

The Importance of the Bride

The symbolic importance of dressing the *zaar* patient as a bride must be emphasized. In this traditional society, as in many others, the one time in her life when a woman is publicly cherished, honored, and made the focus of all concern and attention is when she is a bride. Money is spent by her natal family on her wedding finery and her trousseau, and her husband-to-be provides her with a dowry.[16] Female relatives and friends also devote considerable time and effort to preparing the bride cosmetically for the wedding. She will have all her body hair removed, have her palms, soles, and sometimes legs dyed with henna, have her hair styled, and have makeup applied. Often she is relieved of her work for a time so that she can devote herself to being as attractive as possible for her new husband.

The symbolic and pragmatic aspects of becoming the bride of the *zaar* are thus significant and complex. During a *zaar* ceremony staged in her behalf, a woman can replicate some measure of that singular bridal status. If she is married, she also regains temporarily the implied sexual purity and innocence of the virgin bride. The cultural power of real or implied virginal innocence should not be dismissed. The honor of the family in patrilineal, honor-bound societies is measured in large part by the chastity of the women.

The virgin bride is proof of family honor. The importance of the bride as a symbol of untarnished honor in Nubian society is reinforced when we realize that the rare man who undergoes a *zaar* ceremony is also decked out as a bride.[17] In a society where sexual segregation is severely enforced and male superiority forever touted, a man voluntarily "becomes a woman" only if the status ascribed to that woman is extraordinarily special.

Power and Women

Women in traditional Muslim societies, like those of Egyptian Nubia, like people everywhere, live with stresses that often exact a physical and emotional price. From the moment they are born, girls are made to feel inferior through both social custom and formal Islamic doctrine. Segregation of men and women is severely enforced, and girls are taught to be submissive to males. By Islamic law women inherit half as much as men, and although the formal religion does not prohibit women from attending religious services at the mosque, local practice does. Labial and clitoral excision and infibulation are practiced as ways of making women "clean" and "attractive."

Women have little to say about their marriage partners, and their activities are watched and their chastity guarded. Women have very limited rights to obtain divorce, which can be granted by the Muslim court only in cases of extreme abuse or neglect, but their husbands can divorce them virtually at will. Because it is expensive, polygyny (marriage to more than one wife at the same time) has never been very common, but it is an omnipresent possibility. In recent decades the threat has increased as more and more men migrate to the cities and even overseas for work, not infrequently taking a "city wife" whose existence diverts a large part of the husband's already limited resources. The absent husband also leaves his wife to loneliness and sexual frustration.

For many women (and a few men), becoming possessed by *zaar* spirits is an important way to regain mental and spiritual equilibrium and to encourage or even force other people to take specific actions, at least temporarily. While it is certainly arguable that the energy dissipated in the *zaar* ceremony could be better spent changing the environment so that the ceremonies would be unnecessary, the same point can be (and is) made about various therapies popular in industrial societies. In any case, most individuals are neither able to change their societies nor willing to pay the price of trying to do so. They must find ways to survive within the system in which they live.

The *zaar* system of belief and ritual does not brand the victims of *zaar* as "crazy," but treats them as integral, normal members of the society. Furthermore, it forces people with responsible relationships to the victim—her husband, parents, siblings—to be accountable, ostensibly to the *zaar* spirit but in fact to the woman herself. The *zaar* spirit, speaking through the victim, can demand material goods or attentive, emotionally rewarding actions from those who are made accountable, thus possibly alleviating some of the pressures that brought on the attack. Finally, because possession is not "cured" but rather brought into "remission," *zaar* possession gives the woman the implicit power to become acutely possessed again.

Some critics of the *zaar* see it as a system of formalized extortion used against them by women, bringing the element of belief into some question. Do the women believe they are possessed? Do the *zaar sheikhs* believe in their powers to diagnose the problem and call forth and appease the spirits? Undoubtedly there is no single answer. In Nubia, as elsewhere, there are charlatans and true healers, cynics and saints. There may be women who use the *zaar* to manipulate their husbands just as there are men who use the threat of divorce or polygyny to control their wives. Still, *zaar* spirit possession works within the culture, giving women some limited measure of power to claim the attention, status, and harmony of spirit denied them much of the time.

Notes

1. I have tried to simplify the transliteration of the Arabic words in this article for the convenience of readers who may not be familiar with the usual conventions (i.e., I have done away with diacritical marks denoting Arabic phonemes that do not exist in English). Doubled letters are pronounced "long"—for instance, the double "a" makes *zaar* rhyme with car with the "a" held slightly longer than normal.

2. *Zaar* and similar forms of spirit possession probably originated in Ethiopia, and are also reported in Egypt, Sudan, Ethiopia, and southern Iran.

3. John G. Kennedy, "Nubian *Zar* Ceremonies as Psychotherapy," in *Nubian Ceremonial Life: Studies in Islamic Syncretism and Cultural Change*, ed. John G. Kennedy (Berkeley: University of California Press; and Cairo: American University in Cairo Press, 1978) 203-223.

4. I use the terms "Muslim" and "Islamic" in their Arabic senses to denote different factors. A "Muslim" is a believer in the religion of Islam, and in a "Muslim" society, members consider themselves believers, that is, Muslims. "Islamic" refers to people and cultural elements influenced by Islam; an Islamic society is one heavily influenced by Islam, encompassing not only practicing and secularized Muslims, but also members of other religions.

5. Kennedy, *Nubian Ceremonial Life* 1984.

6. "Telephone" is a children's game. The children sit in a circle. One child whispers a message in the next child's ear, that child in turn whispers in the next child's ear, and so on around the circle. When the message comes full circle, the first child repeats aloud the message she is given, and then the original message. The message as finally transmitted is often significantly different from the original message.

7. The same principle of exclusion applies to all groups to some extent. Outsiders know only what they are allowed to know. To some extent the insiders have no choice, since a great deal of what we learn is not expressed in language and can be described only partially. Watch the interaction among several young children, or among teenagers, and it quickly becomes apparent that they know things we don't.

8. Although the Middle East is considered for theoretical purposes as a single culture area, it is no more culturally homogeneous than is

"the west." Stretching from Morocco to Afghanistan, the Middle East is a mosaic of differing languages, ethnic groups, religions and sects, and sociocultural systems. Thus saying "Muslims believe" something is as problematic as saying "Christians believe" something. Similarly, "Arabs believe" is analogous to "Europeans and North Americans believe." Still, some theoretical generalizations are necessary and, used with care, possible.

9. For a detailed discussion of the psychological and psychiatric implications of the *zaar*, see Kennedy, "Nubian *Zar* Ceremonies."

10. Ibid. 215.

11. In the literature I have seen no one mentions the fact that marrying an already married woman to a *zaar* spirit constitutes polyandry (marriage to more than one man at the same time). Several explanations seem possible—that it's not a concern because of the noncorporeal nature of the second "husband," that the informants haven't thought about it, that the researchers haven't thought about it. In structural terms, the practice may offer some sense of fairness in polygynous Nubian society. In any case, it seems to me an interesting omission.

12. Kennedy, "Nubian *Zar* Ceremonies" 207-208.

13. Ibid.

14. Dr. Hasan El-Shamy, personal communication.

15. Kennedy, "Nubian Zar Ceremonies" 210.

16. Technically, under Muslim religious law, he provides bridewealth, a sum that remains with the woman as her own property, not dowry, a sum taken into a marriage by the bride.

17. Kennedy, "Nubian *Zar* Ceremonies."

WOMEN'S RITUAL
EXPERIENCE

6

Return to the Dance:
The Power of Ritual
in "Ordinary" Lives

Shermie Schafer

ABOVE THE WRITING DESK IN MY HOME HANGS AN ARTWORK BY INDI-
ana artist Dawn Marie Neuenschwander. It is a rendering of
her reflection on Jeremiah 31:13: "Then shall the virgin rejoice
in the dance." It shows a woman—proud, graceful, hair and
scarf flowing, dressed in lavender and purple, laced with a
glint of gold—doing her "dance."

I found this work a decade ago, shortly after completing a
intensive summer seminary course on the prophet Jeremiah.
Every morning for three weeks, I had listened to the railings of
this angry prophet, calling Israel to task. I was particularly
sensitive to the passages referring to Israel as "harlot" and
"whore," and others suggesting that she would be violated
herself for her wanton ways. I felt there were passages supportive (at least psychically) of violence to women, suggesting a
"right place" in which women ought to be kept.

Within weeks I happened upon Dawn Marie's work while
browsing in a local gallery. While the artistic expression of the
piece was beautiful, it was the *spiritual* depth of her "refram-
ing" this image of woman that held me spellbound. I knew
from her work that it was crucial for women to continue to be

involved with and in the Jewish and Christian traditions—finding our own threads in the stories, reclaiming the dignity of the foremothers of our faith-roots. Dawn Marie had offered *me* healing; in some way I knew I needed to add my voice to the efforts toward healing others as well.

A large portion of my fourteen years of ministry has been in the areas of pastoral care and pastoral psychotherapy, as well as marriage and family therapy. I have also served congregations as interim and supply pastor; I have worked with my denominational guidelines committee and professional association ethics committees. I've continued to be involved in women's issues, including those of women and religion. Over the years I've participated in a number of women's groups, including a variety of expressions of WomanChurch. One of these has been the Women's Interfaith Table, an Indianapolis-based group of Jewish, Catholic and Protestant women brought together by common concerns and visions. Our purpose is to discover how our femaleness shapes our faith and how our faith has tried to define our femaleness. We meet quarterly to dialogue, exploring feminist thought and spirituality within these three faith communities. In sharing a common meal, we celebrate the threads of lives in common as well as the blessings of our diversity.

In the context of one of these meetings, Rabbi Sandy Sasso presented a paper on her own experience of writing rituals. I shared with her my idea of creating a healing ritual for victims of abuse, an area of ministry with which I had long been familiar. From that point, we collaborated on the writing of such a ritual, which has since taken on a life of its own.

In addition to the personal enrichment I experienced through my involvement with varied dimensions of Woman-Church, I have continued to feel a call to "the church" in its traditional sense, which has been a major part of my life since infant baptism. Reared in the Lutheran Church-Missouri Synod and a parochial grade school in rural Indiana, I can identify with the faith journeys of others who come from conservative faith backgrounds. As an adult, I have come through a long journey of questioning, reflecting, studying; through anger, agnosticism, seminary, clinical training in psychotherapy and personal therapy. I have been influenced by Jungian studies, mystical experiences, the 12-Step tradition, and my years of working with people in crisis. Ordained a Unitarian Universalist minister in 1984, I now consider myself a mystic-theist and continue to be graced by the diverse ways in which the Mystery of Life itself is revealed to me.

I am personally aware of the power of religion to wound people. The faith tradition in which I was reared in the forties and fifties knew little of the stages of human development; as a child, I was given the same lessons as adults. I now know that such faith teachings have as their goal the surrender of the ego in the second half of life; however, they are counterproductive to the formation of a healthy ego in a child. With a heavy emphasis on one's sinfulness and unworthiness before God, and the exclusivity of God's "chosen" (as was the norm in those days prior to the ecumenical movement), I became an angry, doubting woman . . . and left the church for several years.

By the grace of God and the wisdom of friends, I was led to a female pastoral counselor—Doris Moreland Jones—at age thirty. Here I finally learned of God's grace and love; in her I found a woman whose faith and guidance led me toward the first real healing of those early wounds to my self-esteem. Later events were to show me the love of community, the power of faith in the midst of travail and tragedy, and the reality of a Power greater than myself.

In the course of my ministry, I have worked with many victims of abuse: spiritual and religious, verbal, emotional, physical and sexual. I have heard stories which literally made my stomach turn; it is no surprise to me that so many victims of such abuse develop Multiple Personality Disorder, an attempt of the psyche to survive in the face of such torture.

There have been times in my ministry when my own preaching has been not unlike that of the prophet Jeremiah: full of righteous anger and judgment. Over the years, and through my own experience of grace and healing, I have softened to a point where I am now more focused on bringing healing through a gentler consciousness-raising in others. The healing ritual we created for abused women is such an expression.

In the summer of 1992 Sandy and I were approached by a writer from the *Indianapolis Star*. Someone there had heard of our ritual, and thought it would be an interesting feature for the religion section of the newspaper. Since that time I have received a number of responses to it. Requests for copies have come from

* a retired Baptist clergyman interested in healing;
* the chaplain of the Indiana Boys School, asking permission to adapt it for his population;
* a United Methodist clergyman hoping to adapt it for female victims of abuse in Liberia;
* female professors in various graduate schools throughout the country who hoped to use it with students;
* women suffering from the shame of sexual abuse;
* women's groups in traditional congregations.

I've most powerfully experienced the impact of our healing ritual through the experience of a young woman I'll call "T," who called me after reading the newspaper article. T is a member of a large independent Christian church set in a blue-collar area of this city; the church stationery quotes the scripture verse, "Follow me, and I will make you fishers of men" (Mt 4:19). The church's eight elders, three pastors, and twenty-six deacons are all men. T invited her pastor to join our process as she and I met to explore how the cleansing ritual might be adapted for her within the context of her own faith.

Shortly thereafter I was invited to join T, two of her pastors, and a few close friends from her faith community in the chapel of a local retreat center, where we participated in the ritual T had adapted for the healing of her residual issues of childhood incest. I was moved by the courage of this woman to reach out, speak out, and ask her community for what she needed—in spite of the fact that such a ritual was quite new to them.

The impact of that evening is most eloquently stated in T's own words, written three months after the ritual:

> July 27 was a very special day in my life. For three years I had struggled with the issue of sexual abuse in my life and the effect it had on my relationship with God and others.
>
> My traditional church upbringing had taught me that God was always there, but that didn't help me when I was hurting and searching for answers. When the article on the cleansing ritual appeared in our local newspaper, it was an answer to a prayer. I was at the point in my life where I had been through all types of healing, but I felt that nothing had given my life the renewal and closure that I needed to fully recover and move on . . .

After the ceremony I was left with feelings of hope and renewal. It was like a new birth—being able to put aside my feelings of shame, and being able to forgive. Most of all, I could care for myself and others and let God be a part of my life. That night brought together and aided a very long healing process. I now look at life with greater respect than before, and I care about myself, which I never did before the cleansing ceremony.

Since that evening I have committed myself to working with those who have also been sexually abused, and I have a support group which meets out of my church. At the end of a 14-week recovery process I plan to take each participant through the cleansing ritual.

I know that without the hope and encouragement that the cleansing ritual offered, I wouldn't be telling others about it today. And it should be a sign of hope and healing to all who have suffered the effects of sexual abuse.

Though I've seen T only twice since the ritual, today, six months later, I note a joy and clarity in her voice when we speak on the phone—a very different quality compared to that of the shy, tentative person with whom I first met to discuss the ritual. It is my belief that this was, for T, a transformational event, and that the ritual succeeded in helping T to claim the *self* lost in the violence she experienced as a child.

More recently I have received from T a copy of the brochure that outlines the support group designed by her and one of her pastors for use with other victims of abuse; T has also expressed an interest in making a vocational shift into a ministry that would allow her to focus more on work with such healing. In addition, two of her pastors have sought my consultation regarding ministry to other victims.

It is clear from this case study that this cleansing ritual has had a "ripple effect," not only in T's life, but in the ministry emerging from her pastors' increased awareness of the impact of violence and the need for specific programs and rituals designed to name and heal the effects of such abuse. From a fortuitous article in a newspaper, others have found this ritual a model for further adaptations for healing specific issues in the lives of both women and men. And, not coincidentally, the consciousness of some men has been expanded as well.

The Christian community has long offered *general* prayers for the healing of oppression, stating concerns in global terms;

it has also been more comfortable at times praying for "all those out here" rather than facing the dark truths of those suffering within the local community of faith. Just as frank discussions or ritual inclusions regarding sexuality have traditionally been uncomfortable for the church, so have clergy been slow to name the sins of sexual and domestic violence.

As women have entered more active leadership roles in ministry, we have begun to raise consciousness about women's issues, including dimensions of our sexuality. Whereas men have traditionally done theology out of their minds—intellectualizing concepts and questions about meaning, life, death, and the nature of the divine—women formulate questions and concepts out of their *bodies*. Since the church has traditionally ignored women—in language, leadership, the priesthood, and in naming women's oppression—many have left the church, feeling unworthy of inclusion in community or feeling estranged because their experiences were never given mention.

Traditional theology and liturgy address what are typical white-male "sins": false pride, arrogance and self-absorption, an inflated ego, a grandiose sense of self. Women's "sins" however, are often the opposite: low self-esteem, trivializing one's life and experience, and the inability to form a self. One has to develop an ego before one can surrender it to God, and violence destroys the developing ego of a child, making it impossible for the victim to fully claim her/his birthright as a child of God, worthy of God's grace and redemption.

The cleansing ritual was designed by Rabbi Sasso and myself to fill a gap in liturgical practice: to name the sin of violence; to reconnect women with their collective ancestors as well as their contemporary faith community; to restore "right relationship" between victim and self, victim and others, victim and God. Above all, it was meant to remove the mantle of shame and taintedness and restore the person to her full stature as a child of God (not a "victim"), one who walks again in full dignity and celebration of life.

In my counseling practice, I have at times created rituals to offer closure to issues long struggled with in the therapeutic context. I recall working with a woman who had sought for years to move past her fear of intimacy following an abusive marriage. After two years of participation in a therapy group comprised of both women and men, my male co-leader and I helped her to design a ritual of closure to that episode of her life. One evening she brought to the group a small bag, holding a few symbolic artifacts from that marriage. Together we ventured into an open field, prayed for her release and renewal, burned and buried the remains of the artifacts, and closed with blessings for her new beginning.

More recently, I recall a couple with whom I had worked for months as they struggled to create a more conscious marriage. They had been at the brink of divorce; a lengthy separation, "divorce counseling," and an affair had badly destroyed the trust long taken for granted. The woman had stopped wearing her wedding ring, feeling its symbolic integrity had been destroyed by the events of their last year.

A few days prior to Christmas, I received a call from the husband, telling me he had taken the ring to a jeweler and had designed not only a *new* wedding ring for his wife, but one for himself, in a size and weight with which he felt comfortable. (He had not worn a ring for most of their marriage). He asked if I would help him present this new ring to his wife; I offered instead to create a ritual of recommitment for the two of them.

On the afternoon of Christmas Eve the three of us made our way to the children's chapel in the large church in which I work. We acknowledged the pain, struggle, and work they had endured in order to give new meaning and hope to their marriage; I named the blessing this was for their three young children. They repeated vows to one another, and through tears of new-found joy, placed on each other's hands these new rings symbolic of their transformed marriage.

As we returned to my office and I removed my clerical gown, the woman remarked: "Part of what is so moving for me is that I have never seen a woman robed before! It's just so . . . powerful!"

A month later she called to cancel their counseling appointment with me. "You know," she said, "somehow that ritual just seemed to wash away whatever I thought was left for us to work on. We really don't feel the need to do any more counseling right now. We have decided to buy a new house this year, which I feel will help us with our new start."

This woman's vocation is one of empowering other women. I knew this couple well enough to know that their termination of therapy was not made in denial or resistance, but that in fact the ritual had indeed healed some of their pain and had acknowledged the transcendent grace present to their process. Both are now busy in their mutual vocations as healers and their commitment to creating a healthy family.

In my most recent parish experience as interim minister to a midwest Unitarian Universalist congregation, I performed traditional ceremonies such as weddings and memorial services, as well as union ceremonies and a newer dedication ritual for the blessing of children. In the latter, a service designed to welcome children into the community of faith, I sought to reclaim the use of rich ritual symbols. Since the prayers I choose for worship are often creation-centered, I chose, during the blessing part of the ritual, to touch each child with a smudge of soil, saying these words:

> With earth we remind you of your connection with all life; it is the mother from whom you sprang and it is to her you shall return at the end of your life.

I also chose to reclaim water as part of this ceremony. Since many people attracted to Unitarian Universalist congregations are persons wounded by fundamentalist childhood faith experiences, such reclaiming is a delicate task. As I touched the forehead of each child with water, I said:

> With water we mark this day as your entry upon a spiritual path. May you be sustained and renewed by the Spirit of Life and Love, this day and evermore. Go in peace.

Months later, as I was leaving that interim call, a woman left me a short note, which began with these words:

> So many thanks
> Such a small piece of paper.
>
> Thanks for sharing you with us.
> Thanks for bringing a woman's voice to the Big Room.
>
> Thanks for the Children's Dedication Service,
> individualizing it ever-so-slightly
> for each special new being . . .

I have begun to slowly offer greater use of symbols, realizing that worship must address not only the intellect but the heart, the right-brain as well as the left-brain of participants. A frequent comment about my ministry is that I restore a spiritual dimension to the Sunday services; it is my belief that the gentle expansion of traditional services (in a Unitarian Universalist context) to include more dimensions of ritual and symbolism helped to create that atmosphere for my previous congregation.

My ministry to date has been in "middle America," although that ministry has had varied expressions. While working for four years as a chaplain in a large inner-city hospital and trauma center, my duties included the usual Sunday services, memorial services, and occasional participation in funerals outside the hospital. I also designed blessing ceremonies for the children of nurses, single women who had decided to commit to parenthood without spouses. With families present, I believe these rituals were empowering to these women: naming their courage, blessing their commitment, acknowledging the changing face of "the American family." Such blessing in the context of the extended families adds a spiritual grounding that may not be available for unmarried mothers in traditional churches.

In these ways I have sought to minister through presence, rituals and the re-designing of traditional ceremonies to fit the specific needs of women in their spiritual journeys. Obviously, the average person may not be aware that such a ceremony or ritual might be of value in their journey. For some the word "ceremony" has a safer connotation than the word "ritual," and is more comfortable. If a person arrives at a "stuck point," especially after having done therapy or group work, I may recommend a ritual or ceremony in order to invoke the transcendent dimension, typically not addressed in the average therapeutic context.

Women in ministry have a responsibility to the "average woman" in the "average city" to continue to expand our use of ritual and ceremony to address issues heretofore unaddressed by the traditional church in the healing of both women and men. We need to claim our presence in our communities, in media, in public events, in counseling centers, on community boards, and in worship. We owe that to the large community of faith; such efforts facilitate the continued evolution of the church. Through such involvement in formal and informal connections, we can let others know that we are available for and open to creating rites not addressed in traditional services.

I am reminded of the words of Sister Martha Ann Kirk many years ago, which remain for me a call to involvement in the world:

> Until woman assumes
> her rightful place
> in Christian ministry,
> Christ has only one hand
> with which to heal
> to strengthen,
> to touch,
> and
> to console.[1]

May we continue to assume our rightful place, and in doing so, work with God in restoring others to the Dance which is their rightful inheritance.

Note

1. Janice Grana, ed., *Images: Women in Tradition* (Nashville, TN: The Upper Room, 1976).

7

Ritual as Acceptance/Empowerment and Rejection/Disenfranchisement

Carole A. Rayburn

THE AIM OF THIS PAPER IS TO EXPLORE THE PSYCHOLOGICAL WAYS that religious ritual has been used to define the in- and out-group, to give the "passkey" through ritual to the initiated and to refuse entrance to the "other." Through ritual, traditions are often retained that leave women out and disenfranchise them, while men are accepted and empowered. Ritual allows individuals, traditionally males, to be knighted into the realm of the elite, and the accepted. Ritual within the religious establishment retains and maintains the old boys' network and the male buddy system, while denigrating the sisterhood of women. Women are perceived as incapable of establishing "real" and legitimate traditions and ritual; they may also be seen as interlopers, intruders, trespassers into male ritual whenever they refuse to be excluded any longer.

Since women often have not been allowed by tradition to participate in rites of passage, they often do not think that they need to pay homage to tradition throughout their lives. Basically male rituals, or rituals that accord women unequal and secondary roles, may not only be ill-fitting to women, but may also seem foreign and uncomfortable. Women may see ritual as connectedness, relatedness, and identity with a group of specific others, in addition to a passage to status and power, generating ritual that reflects their creation of life, their creativity in general, their outreach to others, and their nurturing of themselves and others.

For some women, women-church may be the solution, a sanctuary in which they are free to experiment with gender-fitting ritual with other women; there, they need not be fearful of immediate and sure rejection by men who feel threatened by women who want to take part in formerly all-male rituals. In any case, women play many roles and perform various rituals, depending upon the groups to which they belong—both within and outside of the religious establishment—and the comfort that they feel with each group.

In this context, three ritual systems will be examined psychologically here, as they are performed within the Seventh-Day Adventist Church in most of that denomination's religious settings: footwashing, the Lord's Supper or eucharist, and the laying-on-of-hands in ordaining elders and ministers.

Ordinance of Humility (Foot Washing)

The "service (or ordinance) of humility," or footwashing, is a ritual performed in the Seventh-Day Adventist Church about every three months. Whereas footwashing is mentioned in the Old Testament as a rite of hospitality, it is not noted as an ordinance until the New Testament, in John 13:1-14, which records that, just before the feast of Passover, Jesus:

> rose from supper, laid aside his garments, and girded himself with a towel. Then he poured water into a basin, and began to wash the disciples' feet, and to wipe them with the towel with which he was girded. He came to Simon Peter; and Peter said to him, "Lord, do you wash my feet?" Jesus answered him, "What I am doing you do not know now, but afterward you will understand." Peter said to him, "You shall never wash my feet." Jesus answered him, "If I do not wash you, you have no part in me . . . If I then, your Lord and Teacher, have washed your feet, you also ought to wash one another's feet."

All four Gospels speak of the woman who anointed Jesus at

the feast at Simon's house: "weeping, she began to wet his feet with her tears, and wiped them with the hair of her head, and kissed his feet, and anointed them with ointment (Lk 7:38; see also Mt 26:6-14; Mk 14:3-9; Jn 12:1-8).

Ellen G. White, a founder of the Seventh-Day Adventist Church and considered by SDAs to be a prophet, said that

> the ordinance of footwashing is an ordinance of service . . . When this ordinance is rightly celebrated, the children of God are brought into holy relationship with each other, to help and bless each other . . . Christ himself set us an example of humility . . . This lesson does not merely refer to one act. It is to reveal the great truth that Christ is an example of what we through his grace are to be in our intercourse with each other.[1]

Again, several years later, she stated: "This ordinance is to encourage humility, but it should never be termed humiliating, in the sense of being degrading to humanity. It is to make tender our hearts toward one another."[2]

But earlier, White had written:

> The washing of feet and partaking of the Lord's Supper should be more frequently practiced. Jesus set us the example, and told us to do as He had done . . . There is no example given in the Word for brethren to wash sisters' feet, but there is an example for sisters to wash the feet of brethren. Mary washed the feet of Jesus with her tears, and wiped them with the hair of her head. I saw that the Lord had moved upon sisters to wash the feet of the brethren, and that it was according to gospel order.[3]

In practice, footwashing involves gender segregation, with pairs of same-gender persons leaving the sanctuary before the service of the Lord's Supper to wash each other's feet in the ordinance of humility. Men and women, girls and boys, go to different rooms in the church building, each pair getting a pail of water, two towels, and Handiwipes to clean their hands afterwards. Even married couples do not wash each other's feet, there being nothing to prevent this but the custom upholding gender separation.

The only justification given by SDA men for this segregation is that it would be immodest for women to take off their stockings in front of men or, presumably, for men to have to deal with kneeling before a woman's skirt—and perhaps undergarments. This argument does not explain why girls and boys do not wash each other's feet, since all of them usually wear socks, and the girls are generally careful to keep their skirts close to their bodies. Moreover, most women do not shed their pantyhose or stockings, but place their feet in the washbowl or pail with stockings on, and easily towel-dry their feet in seconds.

Since there is no logical reason to segregate females and males for the footwashing, no intrusive aspects into the sexual sensibilities of each gender, what can be the true cause for the gender separation during the service? Pamela Couture has defined rituals as "repeated, normative, symbolic, and functional behaviors often associated with religious expression."[4] She comments on Durkheim's insights on "negative" rituals, which restrain common activities such as words, looks, physical contact, and sexual activity as the individual prepares for initiation into a religious community. "Positive" rituals, on the other hand, mainly concern sacrificial meals and symbolize abundant food production; such rituals reinforce kinship among individuals and renew the ties between people and their god.

Looked at from Couture's perspective, the gender segregation during the footwashing qualifies as a negative ritual from the standpoint of gender, with a perception of restraint of sexual or intimate activity so that individuals can prepare for re-initiation into the religious community.

Victor Turner found that ritual causes communal change, with social intimacy momentarily reversing social roles and status to remind those taking on the power of high status of their connectedness with common people.[5] Certainly, the gender separation does not act to reinforce kinship among males and females. Nor do the limitations on social intimacy of the genders overcome reversal of social roles and status; males, accorded higher social roles and status in our society, seek to wash each others' feet and do not even momentarily wish to symbolically confer gender equality or kinship on females.

Mary Ellen Ross and Cheryl Lynn Ross view ritual as behavior aimed at overcoming separation through community by reconciling differences and bringing absent elements into current interaction.[6] SDA gender segregation surely does not accomplish this.

Lawrence Hoffman speaks of using liturgy to "censor in" a group, whereby the group includes itself in its society's usually accepted definition of proper religiosity. Carving out its places in an "us vs. them" situation, the group then "censors out" other groups in the system to distinguish itself from what it perceives others to be.[7] Censoring out involves preserving the commonly accepted boundaries of the group's religious system by choosing not to accept the cultural values and characteristics of other groups. Hoffman argues further that in our religious communities, even the use of space—the way individuals sit together or sit apart—communicates messages of class and status.[8] Thus, the act of worship is also an act of self-definition, wherein we identify our group and know where we are in it, particularly by the messages that others give to us as to who we are and how we fit in to the group.

SDA males are clearly using the footwashing ritual to censor themselves in to the highest level of acceptance and empowerment in their religious community, while censoring out females and rejecting/disenfranchising them from the same status as male believers. Ironically, even in a ritual that originated as a symbol of humility and service to others, men designate themselves as in a special class, excluding women from the club. Women, taking from the exclusion a poor self-definition and receiving less than inclusive, positive messages from men, get the idea very quickly that they are lower-class citizens in the religious community and fail to fit into the larger group as well as men.

Perhaps, too, after this induction by males of themselves into the realm of the elite, they cannot envision symbolically humbling themselves before women and, thus, placing themselves momentarily in the role of servant or nurturer—a role most decidedly reserved by men for women. Husbands do not even allow themselves to reverse the role that they perceive is theirs—priest of the household—long enough to symbolically give their wives a sense of equality with them in sharing the same home, values, and community.

When men stoop to exclude women on the level of imagined intimacy or sexuality, they are reminiscent of male athletes who want to keep women reporters out of the clubhouse using the excuse that they would not be then able to run around in the nude. What kind of ritual does such freedom for male nudity connote? Is this a rite of spring? Is the complete covering of clothing—and very modest covering it is—the domain and responsibility only of women? Does propriety, along with any other sensibility to others' feelings and thoughts, apply only to one gender?

Women have little chance in gender-separated footwashing of seeing themselves as connected, related to, or identified with the total religious community. In Scripture Jesus says: "If I do not wash you, you have no part in me." Is the very deliberate segregation a way of saying that men and women should not have any part or connection with each other? "I say to you," he goes on, "a servant is not greater than his master": such an instruction wipes away all pretense of inequality before God.

The New Testament describes the widow whom the religious community should take care of:

> Let no one be enrolled as a widow who is under sixty years of age, or has been married more than once; and she must be well attested for her good deeds, as one who has brought up children, shown hospitality, washed the feet of the saints. (1 Tim 5:9-10)

Surely, there is no gender distinction here.

Even Ellen White instructed the church that women should wash the feet of men, as was exemplified for them by Mary Magdalene washing the feet of Jesus with her tears. White stated that this instruction came to her through inspiration and "was according to gospel order." Strangely, this is one inspired teaching that the SDA male hierarchy chooses not to follow. Obviously, the tender-heartedness that White sought only extended among those of matching gender. Perhaps SDA men are in the role of the proud and stubborn disciples who seek to promote themselves (or their gender) for the highest positions in the kingdom,[9] abhorring the role of servant when it means serving women, and avoiding any possibility of reciprocal service with those of different gender.

The footwashing ritual is a preparation for the Lord's Supper, a time of forgiving others and praying for them. Gender seclusion allows believers to forgive and pray only for others of the same sex, those before whom they have humbled themselves. Thus, each gender is only half-prepared for the eucharist. The messages emerging from the same-sex ritual tell of male elitism, exclusivity, acceptance, and empowerment; female punishment and rejection by males; and a sense of failure, or even unworthiness or uncleanness, among women in the company of men.

The Lord's Supper

In the service of the Lord's Supper, women deacons and elders are permitted to bring in the elements—grape juice and bread cubes—and to uncover platters on which each element is served. Once this waitress-like service is performed, however, the women disappear from the scene and the male minister takes over.[10] The male minister thus is the spiritual nurturer/ leader of the community of believers. Men, overriding the teaching of their female prophet, are seen through the male minister in the patriarchal setting of the church as more worthy and powerful than women, related to a male Christ and a God imaged by most male church members as male.

Is it any wonder, then, that women do not sense their empowerment or acceptance, especially when such rituals continually reinforce the idea of female inferiority and inequality? Do men buy the Roman Catholic argument that women cannot possibly be priests or ministers because Christ, the first priest, was a man; women cannot be men; and therefore, women cannot be priests? Do women in an environment with such spiritual restrictions sense that they cannot receive, even symbolically, the body and blood of Christ, because they are female and the embodied Christ was male? And do men really believe this mythological farce?

As Couture pointed out, positive rituals, among which the Lord's Supper would usually be included, primarily involve a sacrificial meal, symbolize abundant food, reinforce relationship among people, and renew ties between all persons and their creator. However, when any group of people comes to the communal table not as family, but as outsiders who are only guests and cannot hope to attain family status (no matter how polite the hosts of the event may be), the meal is for them less meaningful. If women have been excluded in other rituals—even in the prelude leading to the Supper itself—they will have a lingering sense of estrangement that may well transcend their entire worship experience and remain with them in their homes and workplaces.

The picture of Jesus sitting in the upper room with his male disciples around him (the jury is still out as to whether Mary of Bethany/Magdala, that very special person, was truly his first disciple; many would vote in the affirmative) does not fire the female heart and mind with feelings and thoughts of acceptance, rather than mere toleration. As food and drink are given for the nurturing of our bodies, the symbolic bread and wine (or grape juice) of the sacrament of the eucharist nurture the spirit. Women sitting at the Lord's Supper, made to think of themselves in less positive, accepted ways, may regard themselves as less worthy of eating and drinking at the table and may receive less spiritual nourishment than men. If women do take the sustenance offered, they may do so in the role of the servant or maid at the overseers' table. The message from those rituals that accord women second-class status is that men are biologically and spiritually closer to Christ, and thus the only worthy partakers in a fully experienced religious ritual. For women to avoid being permanently devastated by such attempts at rejecting and disenfranchising them, they must be especially strong in confronting misinterpretations of Scripture, ritual, liturgy, and hymns.

Laying-on-of-Hands

The laying-on-of-hands, involving the gifts and rights of an office, has much biblical precedent. Deuteronomy 34:9 says: "And Joshua the son of Nun was full of the spirit of wisdom, for Moses had laid his hands upon him." Acts 6:6, speaking of Stephen, Philip, and others to be set aside for holy service, says: "These they set before the apostles, and they prayed and laid their hands upon them." In Acts 13:3, when Barnabas and Saul were being set aside for God's work, the Scripture says: "Then after fasting and praying, they laid their hands on them and sent them off." 1 Timothy 4:14 commands: "Do not neglect the gift you have, which was given you by prophetic utterance when the elders laid their hands upon you." And 2 Timothy 1:6 says: "I remind you to rekindle the gift of God that is within you through the laying on of my hands."

The laying-on-of-hands is closely related to anointing. In the SDA church, elders or ministers anoint church members with oil when they are dying, very ill, or in need of special spiritual intervention. Male ministers or elders also anoint or consecrate (in the sense of "make or declare sacred") new ministers or elders in a service of ordination. Let us first look at anointing in Scripture, especially as this involves women.

There is some thought that Mary of Bethany is the same person as Mary Magdalene, a sinner and the anointer of Christ at Simon's feast. (Elizabeth E. Platt sees the anointing woman as Mary of Bethany.)[11] Ellen White wrote:

> Mary had been looked upon as a great sinner, but Christ knew the circumstances that had shaped her life . . . Seven times she had heard His rebuke of the demons that controlled her heart and mind . . . in His strength she had overcome . . . The one who had fallen, and whose mind had been a habitation of demons, was brought very near to the Saviour in fellowship and ministry. It was Mary who sat at His feet and learned of Him. It was Mary who poured upon His head the precious anointing oil, and bathed His feet with her tears. Mary stood beside the cross, and followed Him to the sepulcher. Mary was first at the tomb after His resurrection. It was Mary who first proclaimed a risen Saviour.[12]

Suzanne de Dietrich emphasized the messianic significance of Mary's anointing of one who was about to die.[13] Jesus knew that he was to die shortly the death of a criminal, denied customary Jewish burial. To Mary alone God had given this witness of love and faith, putting her in the unique position of representing the incarnate faithful church in the hour of Christ's supreme abandonment. A. Argyle reminded readers that the women who had come to the sepulcher on Easter morning to anoint the body found that Jesus was no longer in the grave.[14] Thus Christ—the Messiah or "anointed one"—was anointed *before* death, and only by the woman Mary.

Platt commented that a major function of Israel's prophets, such as Nathan and Samuel, was to anoint the king's head with holy oil, in much the same manner as they would conduct a royal coronation.[15] In Exodus 28:41 we read about Aaron's sons at their priestly anointing: "anoint them and ordain them and consecrate them, that they may serve me as priests." In carrying out the prophetic office of anointing the king with precious, royal ointment, Mary of Bethany represented Woman standing in the prophetic office for Israel and anointing Christ as Messiah of the House of David. She was the one who prepared Christ's body for crucifixion, death, and burial. In her act of anointing, she establishes a biblical precedent for women's ministry—as ordainers/consecrators, as well as celebrators of the principal ritual of holy communion and preachers of the good news. Mary of Bethany was also the first person to see what even the other disciples had not seen: angels sitting in bright array and the Christ just before his ascension into heaven. In her extraordinary service, Mary was surely a disciple of Christ. If indeed this woman was also the notorious prostitute Mary of Magdala in a time when women seem to have been scapegoated for sexual transgressions simply for being women—even stoned for sins no greater than those of the average man—perhaps not only women, but even "fallen" women were to be allowed places of honor and power, both on earth and in the kingdom.

A few years ago I witnessed an instance of male empowerment and female disenfranchisement which lingers in my memory like a deep, unhealed wound. While I was experiencing feelings of sorrow and anger at the unfolding ritual, I was also, as a professional psychologist, observing others in the congregation. A man who had never served as a minister nor been ordained was hired out of a church publishing job to be the minister of one of the largest and most influential (and, in relative terms, most progressive) SDA churches. On his first sabbath at the church, he was both ordained into ministry and welcomed into the church as its minister. In the sanctuary around the pulpit were assembled the incoming minister and some ten male elders who had been invited to form a circle around him for the ritual laying-on-of-hands of ordination.

Also present was a woman who had been an associate in pastoral care at the church for several years. The church had permitted her to baptize a few people whom she was instructing in the faith, but this was a special *ad hoc* permission that was not approved by the highest church authorities. She had read Scripture as background for the male minister's sermon and had made a call for the offering, and was thus at the pulpit when the male elders were invited to lay their hands on the new man. But she visibly winced at the call, because she knew that she was not to be included among those elders. Ironically, she had been ordained an elder in another SDA church, but though she had transferred that office to the current church, there was no entitlement for her to lay hands on the new pastor. Throughout the ceremony, her visage remained sad and disturbed.

I remember recoiling at the irony of the situation, wondering how anyone could think that a just God and loving Savior would ever condone such treatment of one-half of God's people and over sixty percent of the denomination. Many other women in the church were also flinching and squirming in their seats. Both the woman minister and the women in the congregation appeared to be experiencing both embarrassment and shame—and the hot flash of exclusion by the men in power. Certainly, such a lack of loving kindness would not enrich the kinship ties of women and men in the congregation. What would have otherwise been a beautiful and meaningful spiritual ritual became a hideous symbol of rejection which left a bitter taste in the soul.

Whether the male elders sensed any remorse or sorrow over this exclusion of their associate, I don't know, but they could not help but sense their own entitlement, acceptance, and empowerment as they—and not any women—were chosen to serve in the ritual of inducting yet another of their kind into high church office. Undoubtedly, some, or even many, of them were insensitive to the plight of the woman, even oblivious to the fact that she was still physically nearby, seated on a chair behind the circle of the brethren. But it should have come as no surprise that, when the woman decided to give up her position in the SDA church about a year later, she also left the denomination of which she had been a lifelong member and joined another church that allowed her to be a clergywoman with all the clerical rights of that office.

For many of the women present that day, the pain was intense. The just-below-the-surface sting was something that few would have chosen to deal with on a more conscious level. The resulting confrontation could well have run out of control, the bitterness of disempowerment going too deep and causing too much anger to be released all at once. At such times denial is a truly meaningful defense mechanism, since it saves the individual from waging a battle with the oppressor and risking losing even more in the fight. Here, though, the men had gone too far, and more than one woman was noticeably wounded. The incident was galvanizing, however. What may have been intended as a ritual celebrating membership in the elite male club of ministry had backfired, and may have strengthened women to fight future battles.

Many SDA men have justified gender discrimination in the church for years by noting that "women are naturally more religious than men, and so men must be given more incentives to join the church and to keep coming to services." The absurdity of this argument is obvious: men are psychologically rewarded for being less spiritual and faithful to the community! The harder work of women in their churches nets them fewer rewards than men, because male elders are considered "bigger catches" by the male power structure than women.

Scripture is not without examples of women taking full part in the rituals of the faithful: footwashing, anointing (even Christ himself), preaching, teaching, evangelizing, discipling by definition and function. What is not happening enough is women reclaiming or claiming acceptance—beginning with self-acceptance and self-worth—and empowerment. As long as churchwomen wait for churchmen to bestow upon them a sign of approval and acceptance, they are not in control and are relinquishing any real claim to spiritual maturity and equality of gender.

* * * * * *

This paper is an attempt to begin the important task of uncovering the dynamics of the interface of women and religious ritual, an area which—particularly in its psychological aspects—has been barely investigated. In fact, it has only been relatively recently that the psychological concerns of religious women have been the focus of study. In beginning to scratch the surface, I have found that clergywomen of many denominations have seen themselves, both in seminary and the parish, as rejected and viewed with suspicion by their colleagues and congregants, and as "going against the tide" in working in a field traditionally reserved for men.[16]

Religion has promoted the value of individual acceptance within the community of believers as the highest level of human striving. From such acceptance, it has taught, all other empowerment for the religious person is generated. Ritual serves to reinforce the initiation and continuance of loyalty ties to the group, making group identity strong and long-lasting. When women are treated differently and in ways which reject and disenfranchise them in rituals, they become frustrated, confused, fearful of rejection and loss of self-esteem, sorrowful, angry, prone to avoid looking head-on at the problem, and apt to deny (at least initially) what is actually happening. If women have been encouraged through ritual to believe they are inferior and lack power within the religious community, they usually will transfer this poor self-image to other settings—home, work-place, and other communities. They will strive for little because they will have a deep sense of worthlessness and potential failure about what they attempt. To accept such rejection, they must deny their feelings of fear and anger and defend their fear of being further rejected should they try to change their one-down position. They will avoid all evidence in conflict with their subservience.

Women in more positive environments and those who begin to question their oppressive situation may avoid their oppressors and the negativity around them; they may also avoid contact with those in the same situation. There may well be a schizophrenic-like split between their "good selves" in a self-fulfilling and self-enhancing environment (home, work, other religious settings) and their "bad selves" in the unaccepting surroundings in which ritual is counterproductive. Such women may, like persons with dual citizenship, have to relate to each of the groups to which they belong in different ways, since in one group, their citizenship would be only marginal. The controlling male group takes for granted that women will be psychologically confused and unaware of having been cut off from full participation in the group. Women thus find themselves in a double bind: on the one hand, they are treated as less valuable than others in the group—assumed to be less spiritual, less at one with the creator, less skillful in pastoral care, less perceptive; on the other, they are encouraged to deny whatever insights of intelligence and understanding they might bring to bear in analyzing their situation and seeking greater acceptance. Most destructive is the strong possibility that, through negative religious ritual, women are rewarded when they "know their place"; thus, they do not learn to achieve and gain equality with men. And since ritual reinforces keeping women and girls in subservient positions, leadership training within the *ecclesia* is almost nonexistent. Unable to trust their own feelings, they become increasingly dependent upon men in parent-child interaction.

Women may also be confused by misinterpretations of Scripture advanced to back up negative ritual roles for females, and may think that only men can progress in education, business, and so on, and that the parental/patriarchal teaching authority of the religious establishment does not and will not work to further the psychological and spiritual development of women, as it does for men. They are understandably confused when their disenfranchisement is presented as part of divine will. And when the patriarchy claims that its negative rituals are meant to protect women in the name of love, women grow to distrust their own perceptions and feelings, and to distrust others—especially men.

If, on the other hand, women overadapt to male expectations, achieving less to please men, they will learn to fail in other areas of life; to become male clones, taking pride in keeping other women from venturing into their restricted field; or to play psychological games that keep them from knowing who they really are or what they could have achieved. They will not be self-actualizers, but mere extensions of men, living in psychological states of depression, suspicion, anxiety, hopelessness and, often, anger. The message for women is that failure is so inevitable that trying to accomplish anything valuable would be foolish and delusory. Their ability to free their creative selves deteriorates over time from lack of use or misuse. Women eventually mislearn or unlearn those life lessons that would best prepare them to function optimally as equals with men.

In order for women not to suffer stunted spiritual, educational, and psychological growth, they must be willing to accept themselves as worthy beings striving for spiritual adulthood. They need to speak for themselves and to make rules and rituals that accommodate their own needs, thoughts, and feelings. They must define themselves, not allow men to do this. The result can be more egalitarian, meaningful, and empowering ritual for both women and men. When this is accomplished, women as well as men, religion and society will be richer, more productive, and more self-actualized. Healthier psyches and spirits will then prevail.

Notes

1. E.G. White, *Manuscript 43* (Mountain View, CA: Pacific Press, 1897).

2. E.G. White, *Review and Herald* 75:22 (31 May 1898): 1.

3. E.G. White, *Early Writings* (Washington, D.C.: Review and Herald, 1882).

4. Pamela Couture, "Ritual and Pastoral Care," in *Dictionary of Pastoral Care and Counseling*, ed. R.J. Hunter, H.N. Malony, L.O. Mills, and J. Patton (Nashville: Abingdon Press, 1990).

5. Victor Turner, *The Ritual Process* (Cornell, NY: Cornell University Press, 1969).

6. M.E. Ross and C.L. Ross, "Mothers, Infants, and the Psychoanalytic Study of Ritual," *Signs: Journal of Women in Culture and Society* 9 (1983): 26-39.

7. Lawrence Hoffman, "Censoring In and Censoring Out: A Function of Liturgical Language," in *Ancient Synagogues: The State of Research*, ed. J. Gutman (Ann Arbor, MI: Scholars Press) 19-37.

8. Lawrence Hoffman, "Assembling in Worship," *Worship* 56 (1982): 98-112.

9. White discusses this behavior in *Desire of Ages* (Mountain View, CA: Pacific Press, 1940).

10. There are no clergywomen in the SDA Church; no women are ordained as ministers, nor do they enjoy the salary, title, or status of clergymen. Women working on the church staff, preaching, and doing pastoral counseling or other ministerial tasks are entitled "associates in pastoral care."

11. E.E. Platt, "The Ministry of Mary of Bethany," *Theology Today* 34 (1977): 29-39.

12. White, *Desire*.

13. S. de Dietrich, *The Layman's Bible Commentary: Matthew* (Richmond, VA: John Knox, 1961).

14. A.W. Argyle, *Cambridge Bible Commentary: The Gospel According to Matthew* (Cambridge: Cambridge University Press, 1963).

15. Platt, "The Ministry of Mary."

16. C.A. Rayburn, L.J. Richmond, and L. Rogers, "Men, Women, and Religion: Stress within Leadership Roles," *Journal of Clinical Psychology* 42:3 (1986): 540-546.

WOMEN'S RITUAL EXPRESSION

8

Ritual Creedal Language and the Statement of Faith of the Evangelical Women's Caucus[1]

Linda Coleman

THERE IS A TENSION BETWEEN THE SUPPOSEDLY "NORMAL" FUNCTION of language—to communicate information—and its use in ritual, where maintaining a predictable structure may be more important than communicative efficiency. The point can be illustrated with a commonplace example. Competent members of American culture know that the correct response to the conversation opener, "How are you?" is "Fine, thank you. How are you?" or something very close to it. We may play limited variations on that theme ("I'm well, thanks. And yourself?"), but we know that the one thing we may not do is give an accurate account of our state of health. People who respond with real communication rather than the ritually established reply are usually not asked that question again.

Similarly, court sessions are opened with a bailiff crying "Oyez!" three times, rather than, say, "Attention, please!", not because "oyez" is a more accurate way to tell people to attend to the proceedings or because the addressees are so rowdy that they need to hear it three times, but because it is sanctioned by tradition. The value in its continued usage is that those present are reminded that they are participating in an event that has been carried out in much the same way for a long time, that what they are doing has the force of history, as well as of present authority, behind it.

In the case of religion, in particular, we see this tension between a focus on *what* is said and *how* it is said. On the one hand, religious utterances, such as those in the liturgy, are supposed to map onto reality. Indeed, there is a presumption, tacit or otherwise, that religious things are said a certain way not only because that is the expected way to say them, but because it is the way to say them truthfully. Religious utterances are supposed to present the truth about transcendental matters, as far as it can be presented in human language.

Yet truthfulness is not the only standard. When a particular form has long been accepted as the way to talk about God, any change in that form will engender resistance, even a change that improves the accuracy of the communication for the modern audience. Some traditionalists, for example, insist that it is best to read the Bible in King James English and to address God in prayer as *thou* because it raises the level of formality and clearly distinguishes the forms of those utterances from those of everyday speech. This argument ignores the fact that originally *thou* functioned as the informal pronoun, and that in other European languages with second person formal/informal distinctions, God is customarily addressed with the informal pronoun. But what has happened is entirely natural: speakers have become accustomed to a certain type of language and, when its use is threatened, they creatively find rationales for retaining it that had nothing to do with the intent behind its original use.

The tendency not only to retain older forms but to justify those forms as having somehow achieved the "right" level of truthfulness creates special problems for women who are interested in non-traditional roles in religious practice. As Marjorie Procter-Smith observes, the ritual and theological language sanctioned by tradition is male-based and treats women as the adjuncts of men—that is, invisible—but by doing so "makes the truth of whatever is said suspect, since women are in fact not invisible."[2]

When dealing with the ritual language of religion, therefore, we have the requirements, on the one side, that the language be within the range of what is expected and sanctioned by tradition, and, on the other, that the language must accurately communicate the truth. We can add to these a third feature of ritual language: the ability to use the language correctly marks the user as a member of the community.

To explore that interface between language and ritual, and specifically to look at what happens when all three of those features—the belief in accuracy, the need for the expected, and the membership-marking function—interact, I will examine the creation of a ritual piece of language—the creedal statement of a new religious organization.

It is a mistake to regard the composition of any creed as merely a matter of selecting essential beliefs and listing them with the appropriate stylistic flourishes. Much more goes on, including some very deep thinking about the very nature of a creedal statement, and the particular aim of the one in question.[3] The case we shall look at, however, is more complicated yet, for the creed marked the formation of a feminist group, the Evangelical Women's Caucus (EWC), within the conservative evangelical Christian tradition. The writers' complex task was to make use of traditional linguistic forms to establish their theological *bona fides*, while simultaneously expressing their identity as feminists in a conservative environment.

To understand the context in which the statement of faith was written, we will begin by looking at the history of the EWC itself and then at the special features of language use that mark evangelical orthodoxy.

Evangelicals and Feminists

We need to define at the outset what is meant by "evangelical." Terms like "evangelical," "fundamentalist," and "liberal" are often used so confusingly that it is easy to forget that they are clear enough to those to whom they refer. The terms "evangelical," "evangelistic," and "fundamentalist" are particularly prone to be used improperly as synonyms.

Some of the confusion stems from the significant overlap among these broad groupings of Protestant Christians. When trying to define these terms, then, we do best to think of them as representing a series of overlapping ranges on a continuum from conservative to liberal, rather than as discrete units. Charismatics, for example, reside in a great many denominations. Indeed, a denomination may span more than one category—there *are* evangelical Episcopal churches, and very Catholic ones, although generally Episcopalians are considered mainline-to-liberal. On the conservative end of the scale, we can locate evangelicals between mainline churches (like the United Methodists, the Presbyterians, Congregationalists, and most Lutherans), on the one hand, and the fundamentalists on the other.

Christianity Today, a popular evangelical magazine, defines evangelicals as those holding strong, orthodox Protestant beliefs based on a conversion experience (being "born again") in which they acknowledged Jesus Christ as uniquely the Son of God and accepted him as their personal savior.[4] In addition, evangelicals typically believe that the Bible is the inspired word of God, that it does not contain errors (although some of its language may be figurative or illustrative), that the human race began when God created Adam and Eve, and that after death humans will go either to heaven or to hell.

Whereas many conservative beliefs, such as the insistence upon being "born again," unite evangelicals and fundamentalists, evangelicals as a group tend to hold rather more liberal positions than fundamentalists. For example, evangelicals are more likely to allow that not all of the Bible is to be taken as instruction and that some of its material may be limited in application to the first hearers. They may accept metaphorical interpretations or other broad readings of some portions of the Bible.

Churches and the individuals in them are very clear about where they fit on this continuum, and organizations such as the National Association of Evangelicals and Evangelicals for Social Action have a clear and self-identified constituency.[5]

Religious conservatism so often goes with social conservatism that many people are surprised to hear of evangelical feminists. However, in the last century, many of the suffragists were also extremely religious—and religiously conservative—people, and the Women's Christian Temperance Union, to name only one organization, was deeply concerned with women's rights.[6] But in more recent times, evangelical churches have as a rule taken a conservative stance on the role of women in the church, as well as in society at large, a stance which generally limits women's occupation of leadership positions, and which focuses on their traditional roles as supporters of male initiative and leadership.

Since the early 1970s, however, a feminist movement has been finding its place within evangelicalism. The "Chicago Declaration" issued in 1973 by the new organization, Evangelicals for Social Action, identified patterns of male "prideful domination" and female "irresponsible passivity" as common—and deplorable—among conservative Christians.[7]

The task force formed by Evangelicals for Social Action to study women's issues soon gathered steam and became a national organization called the Evangelical Women's Caucus, holding its first national conference in 1975.[8]

The Language of Evangelical Christianity

One sign of being a competent member of a group, whether lawyers, college students, or evangelical Christians, is knowing how to *talk* like a member of the group. This means not merely knowing the meanings of ritualized terms, but also being able to manipulate the rhetorical patterns of the group "language."

As I have pointed out elsewhere,[9] there exists something that we might, for convenience, call the "language of evangelical Christianity," a range of speech behaviors that includes the use of specialized terminology, rules of politeness, and a tendency towards certain syntactic patterns.[10] Thus, for example, terms like *minister to [someone]* are not generally found in ordinary secular speech, and even among evangelicals are limited to contexts in which the speaker wants to emphasize the religious nature of the activity. Consider the difference between three apparently synonymous sentences:

1. Janet really helped us.
2. Janet was really there for us.
3. Janet really ministered to us.

All three examples describe the same kind of event: Janet has done something to help the speaker. But in each case, the phrasing suggests a different view of the situation. The first sentence is what we might consider the "normal" or, in linguistic terms, "unmarked," form. There is no clue as to what kind of help was provided, why it was needed or how either the speaker or Janet felt about the act(s) involved in helping. In the second sentence, by contrast, we have language often associated with counseling. The phrasing *to be there for N* is likely to occur when the focus is on N's (probably short-term) emotional incapacity. The kind of help given in (2), then, is usually moral support or the equivalent (Janet listened while we talked through our grief). If it is something practical like mowing the lawn, the implication is that help was needed because of some emergency: Janet mowed the lawn because we were spending all our time at the hospital with a dear friend. One does not use the phrasing in (2) to recommend Janet to a neighbor as someone who has shown herself to be a highly skilled landscaper.

Sentence (3) evokes a specifically religious reading of the event. Whatever Janet did, it was perceived as a service performed on behalf of God for the speaker. Our first thought when we hear the sentence may be that Janet offered spiritual counsel, but it may equally well be used to report simply that Janet preached at a normal church service. However, since any action, including mowing the lawn, may be done as part of a believer's service to God, the decision to use religiously marked language may establish a religious context for an action which is not in itself inherently religious.

Not all ritualized evangelical terms are religious in meaning. Language typical of the King James version of the Bible suffices to bring out a religious context for any utterance. For example, the use of the word *rejoice* in the sentence, "I rejoice in the good weather we're having," though uncommon in ordinary speech, is recognizable as typical of this kind of language. Although rejoicing is not in itself inherently religious, the use of the word signals that the speaker is not merely happy about the weather, but is thinking of the weather in religious terms—that is, expressing gratitude specifically to God for arranging for a fine day.

Since evangelicals are expected to be thoroughly familiar with the Bible, the biblical text itself constitutes a ground of shared knowledge which may be evoked by a word or phrase. References to "spiritual warfare," for example, go beyond the simple metaphor, "argument is war,"[11] to bring to the evangelical's mind an entire scheme after Ephesians 6:11-17, in which various spiritual practices are described as pieces of armor, and the sole offensive weapon is the Bible, the "sword."

There is, then, a "language of evangelicalism," much as there is a "language of the law" and a "language of medicine." In the case of evangelicals, this language includes (1) terminology that refers specifically to religious actions (*minister to*), (2) the availability of what might be considered a distinct register, or style—that of the King James Bible, and (3) a shared body of knowledge, the Bible, which forms the backdrop for any communication about religious matters.

Evangelicals themselves are very aware of their specialized language, and their choice of unmarked or religious forms is thoughtful and deliberate. Hence, for example, the recognition during the 1992 presidential campaign of the ability of Democratic candidates Clinton and Gore to, as one Southern Baptist put it, "speak the language I speak." He went on to analyze the effect of this rhetorical practice: "By intentionally using that language, they are affirming that [religious] tradition . . . [t]hey interpret liberal concepts in language that speaks to us Bible Belters."[12]

As with the specialized languages of medicine and the law, competence in the use of "evangelical language" serves as one way of identifying someone as theologically orthodox. It is especially important for evangelical feminists to be able to use the language this way, because they are often accused of merely aping secular feminists, with no biblical justification for their position. Indeed, *Uplook*, a magazine published by a conservative branch of the Plymouth Brethren, objected recently to an advertisement published by a newer evangelical feminist organization, Christians for Biblical Equality, remarking that "[i]ts statements are neither couched in the language of the Bible nor supported by actual quotations from the Bible."[13] The value of using the "right" religious language as a marker of shared identity is clearly strong enough to allow an organization's failure to use such language to be presented among the reasons for denying that organization the recognition one extends to brother and sister Christians.

Creedal Statements in Evangelicalism

It should be apparent that evangelical feminists face an interesting problem in constructing their statements of faith. One displays competence by using the language correctly; however, most of the terminology relevant to the place of women in Christian theology is based on a highly patriarchal interpretation. Refusal to use the traditional language would undercut the writers' authority as orthodox Christians, but using terms in their traditional senses undercuts their own position. And, because the evangelical audience is expected to be familiar with the biblical passages relevant to women and their roles, simply ignoring the traditional patriarchal interpretations won't work, either. The audience will expect some treatment of such significant—and problematic—concepts as the notion of *headship*.

A statement of faith can be a very serious business in evangelical circles. Certainly, the creation of a creedal document is an important issue for a new church, but even more so for a parachurch organization, since the latter organization's acceptability to the churches attended by its potential membership is not a foregone conclusion. The statement of faith becomes, then, something of a passkey for the organization, a point made aptly by Lawrence Hoffman:

> every group both includes itself in its society's generally accepted definition of licit religiosity and at the same time, carves out its own niche within the system, defining what it is that differentiates "us" from "them." I call the former process "censoring in"; the latter, "censoring out."

> Religious identity is the composite of these two processes. Even as we censor others out by assuring our members that we are different, we censor ourselves into our society's definition of acceptable religiosity.[14]

This holds true especially for organizations within the evangelical movement, where a variety of denominations and individual churches co-exist independently. With no central authority to rule on whether an organization is within the range of orthodoxy, the statement of faith becomes a test: if the statement of faith is acceptable, the producer(s) of the statement must also be accepted as orthodox, and those who cannot quarrel with the statement of faith must be willing, in evangelical terms, to be in fellowship with those who produced and agree with the statement.

There have been many discussions of the function of the class of text that includes the liturgical creed and the written statement of faith. Ritual creedal statements have, historically in Christianity, been descriptive, confessional, baptismal affirmations of faith (early church and Apostles' Creed); dogmatic theological statements (Nicene and Athanasian Creeds); and didactic institutional definitions (Protestant confessions). Some creedal statements list just those items of faith that the group considers essential in "censoring itself in": those shared with everyone else the group regards as Christian—hence Rufinus' comparison of the creed with military uniforms or passwords which enable group members to recognize each other, and presumably to deal effectively with outsiders trying to pass as group members.[15] Other creeds have a different focus: although they usually include enough description of basic doctrines to establish the identity of the group, their emphasis is on specifying those areas where the group differs from other Christian groups.[16]

The EWC statement of faith, understood in the classic Protestant sense as definitional and didactic, must do both jobs: it must show how *this* Christian organization differs from others, but at the same time evangelical feminism must be presented as well within the range of orthodoxy. Indeed, it must communicate, however subtly, that, from the feminist perspective, the traditional patriarchal interpretation of certain Christian doctrines is incorrect, and point the way to another position. The writers have accomplished this difficult task by creative use of the ritual language of evangelicalism.

Analysis of the Statement of Faith

The writers have made use of traditional terminology, using standard terms on undisputed matters—remember that both authors and addressees are evangelicals, so there is a great deal of common ground—but redefining or co-opting those pieces of the terminology strongly associated with a patriarchal stance.

While the text is full of standard religious terms—*in the divine image, fellowship, sinful disobedience, right relationship with God, the Incarnation, truly divine and truly human, personal relationship, Savior and Lord,* and so on—it is worth noting the structure in which that language occurs. Paragraphs 1, 4, 6, and 7 are entirely acceptable within a traditionalist framework, and contain almost no uniquely feminist features, except for the avoidance of male-oriented language. Sandwiched between these ostensibly innocuous segments, however, are paragraphs that make very important points for the feminist perspective, but that present those points in language which does not invite dispute by traditionalists. Although the writers make use of traditional schemas, such as the Fall or church organization, the focus is on elements that are less salient in more traditional views. A closer examination of the statement of faith shows how traditional and feminist features are combined.[17]

PARAGRAPH 1:

We believe that God, the Creator and Ruler of all, has been self-revealed as the Trinity.

This paragraph could stand as part of a traditional Evangelical statement of faith. Here it establishes the *bona fides* of the writers. It is a feature of the traditional creedal statements (the Nicene, Apostles' and Athanasian Creeds, for example) that they consist of a sequence of paragraphs with generally consistent structure, each beginning with "I [or *we*] believe." This statement varies slightly, but acceptably, from those creeds in substituting a *that*-clause in place of the expected prepositional phrase with *in* ("We believe in God the Father Almighty . . ."). By setting up a *that*-clause as the expected next element in each paragraph, the writers prepare the reader for statements of action—beliefs that something has happened or should happen—rather than the more static, and more customary, beliefs *in* something.

It is worth noting as well that a few things that might appear in a traditional creed have been left out. There is, of course, no sex-definite reference to God—"the Father". In addition, the passive, *has been self-revealed as the Trinity*, is peculiar, but neatly avoids the need for a gender-definite pronoun—*God has revealed Himself as the Trinity*. The preference among Christian feminists is to repeat *God* in place of pronouns, but *God has revealed Godself as the Trinity* would bring into prominence one important difference between feminist and traditional views and so would unnecessarily offend traditionalist readers.

The absence of any definition of *Trinity* presupposes a Christian audience or at least an audience familiar with Christian doctrine.

PARAGRAPH 2:

We believe that God created humankind, female and male, in the divine image, for fellowship with God and one another. We further believe that because of human sinful disobedience, the right relationship with God was shattered, with a consequent disruption of all other relationships.

Here, no disputed theological points are raised, and there is little to cause comment or surprise, except for the term *humankind*, normally *mankind* in traditional evangelical terms, and the ordering of *female and male*. That ordering harks back to the sequencing in Genesis 1:27: "So God created man in his own image, in the image of God created he him; male and female created he them."[18] That ordering is ambiguous.

One reading is that God created the entire human race in the divine image, with the subsequent mention of "male and female" simply serving to include both sexes in the creation. However, that verse has sometimes been taken, in conjunction with 1 Corinthians 9:7, "[the man] is the image and glory of God: but the woman is the glory of the man," to mean that only Adam was truly created in God's image. The ordering in the EWC statement disambiguates in favor of the first reading, including the female as a creation in the divine image.

Not surprisingly, *in the divine image* replaces the more traditional *in His own image*, again avoiding the masculine pronoun.

The second sentence brings us almost back to a fully traditionalist statement, with two exceptions: *human sinful disobedience* replaces the more common *man's sinful disobedience*. The redundant term *sinful disobedience* places the authors not only squarely within evangelical theology, but also squarely within the traditional style of talking about theology. *Right relationship with God* is also straightforward, traditional evangelical phraseology.

While this paragraph is ostensibly about humanity's destroyed-and-now-restored relationship with God—exactly what would be expected in a traditional statement of faith—the final phrase introduces an equivalent claim about inter-human relationships, which paves the way for the following argument: if the breach with God had as a consequence disruption of inter-human relationships, and if that breach was healed by the death of Jesus Christ, then, reasonably enough, the inter-human relationships should likewise be healed, or made ready for healing, in the same way, and, importantly, at the same time. This argument responds to a belief that, while women became subordinate as a result of the Fall (see Gn 3:16), they will be restored to equality only in heaven, where there are no sex distinctions in any case. By tying together as synchronous the healing of inter-human relationships and the healing of the breach with God, the statement suggests that, upon conversion to Christianity, humans should be prepared to reject the subjection of women that resulted from the Fall as they reject their pre-conversion patterns of sinful thinking and behavior.

PARAGRAPH 3:

We believe that God in love has made possible a new beginning through the Incarnation, in the life, death and resurrection of Jesus Christ, who was, and is, truly divine and truly human.

After the mention of the Fall, we expect a reference to the redemption, and here it is. This one closely follows the normal form of such a statement, with the more modern *truly divine and truly human* replacing the older phrasing *truly God and truly man*.

The phrase, *a new beginning*, serves here to evoke the idea that changes should be expected in every facet of a Christian's behavior, and thus it prepares the reader further for the suggested change in male-female relationships hinted at above. It harks back, as well, to the previous *disruption of all other relationships*, suggesting that male-female relationships as they currently stand are not within the original divine plan, but are the result of sin. Again, by implication, equality of the sexes must be part of the redemption.

Another point of interest is the absence of a ritually important phrase: Jesus Christ in such a context as this often appears as *His Son, Jesus Christ*. The omission is not noticeable, I have found, unless one is looking for it, and so does not constitute any sort of red flag. Omitting it does, however, solve a problem for the writers, since, on the one hand, they cannot include it in its traditional form without using exclusive language and gender-specific references to God, but, on the other hand, they cannot use a form more acceptable to themselves (for example, *God's Child, Jesus Christ*) without losing traditionalist readers.

The omission here marks the EWC statement's departure from more traditional creeds, in which the members of the Trinity are described in familial terms, *Father, Son and Holy Spirit*. The EWC's focus is less on the relationship between the members of the Trinity and more on that between humanity and God.

PARAGRAPH 4:

We affirm a personal relationship with Jesus Christ as Savior and Lord.

This is standard evangelical phrasing. However, it is worth noting that the EWC reflects the (probable) greater liberalness of its constituency by being a bit more ecumenical than many evangelical groups. Evangelicals, as noted above, tend to focus on a single conversion experience, being "born again." The experience is described as "accepting Jesus Christ as one's personal Savior" and is seen as the start of a personal relationship with Jesus Christ. Whereas mainstream churches may include within their theology the idea of a personal relationship with Christ, they tend to put less emphasis on the specific occasion on which the relationship begins. Here, it is worth noting, the EWC insists upon the relationship, but does not demand that it begin at an identifiable instant.

The use of *Lord* here is the one gender-specific term used of the Deity in this statement, and worth some attention for that reason. The term has been the subject of debate among Christian feminists, with some writers and translators choosing to replace it with other alternatives, such as *sovereign*. Nancy Hardesty notes that just such a debate occurred shortly after this statement was published, with defenders of the term suggesting that, since it is no longer regularly used of human males, at least in American society, it arguably does not give God an identity based on a male-centered metaphor. In that respect, *Lord* differs from terms like *Father*. Hardesty comments:

> During the 1983 Bicentenniel Consultation on Wesleyan Theology and the Next Century at Emory University, the feminist theology group discussed the issue. Rosemary Radford Ruether reminded us that the initial theological intent of the affirmation that Jesus Christ is Lord was to say that Jesus is God and no one else is. The martyrs died because they considered Jesus to be God, but they did not believe any emperor who proclaimed himself divine, to be God. Thus to say that Jesus Christ is Lord is precisely to affirm that no man, no human being, is. Therefore, for today's woman the affirmation that Jesus Christ is Lord can be precisely the same kind of attack on patriarchal structures as it was for the early Christians.[19]

In this case the tension between the ritually familiar term and a gender-neutral alternative is resolved with an assist from the word's historical use. The equally ritually familiar *Father* is generally eliminated in favor of an inclusive alternative.

In the 1990 revision of the EWC statement of faith, this paragraph was dropped altogether.

PARAGRAPH 5:

We believe that under Christ's headship and through the work of the Holy Spirit we are freed to exercise our gifts responsibly in our churches, homes and society.

The radical use of standard evangelical terminology is focused within this paragraph. The first and most obvious usage shift is the term *headship*, associated in traditional thought with a very specific pattern, described in St. Paul's Letters to the Corinthians and the Ephesians: "But I would have you know that the head of every man is Christ; and the head of the woman is the man; and the head of Christ is God" (1 Cor 11:3). "Wives, submit yourselves unto your own husbands, as unto the Lord. For the husband is head of the wife, even as Christ is the head of the church: and he is the saviour of the body. Therefore as the church is subject unto Christ, so let the wives be to their own husbands in every thing" (Eph 5:22-24). These verses have led, in traditional theology, to the creation of a kind of "chain of command": God→Christ→man→woman. Indeed, in evangelical writings it is rare to find a mention of the term *headship* that does not refer to the male-female relationship.

Here, however, the writers have created an alternative emphasis, and one that is also well within traditional theology: all Christians, as members of the church, are under Christ's headship. This phrasing co-opts the loaded term *headship* and evokes an alternative image of the church that conservatives agree with, although they do not give it the emphasis they give male headship: that all members of the church, men as well as women, must be equally subject to Christ, and that God may reveal his will to women as well as to men.

Curiously, this phrasing opens up another can of worms. As it stands, and in this context, it would seem to suggest that Christ serves as an authority figure over both male and female members of the church—the emphasis is on the position of both "under Christ's headship." However, evangelical feminist scholars have argued as well that *head* does not refer in the Greek to an authority figure, but to an origin or source of strength.[20] While it is true that the preferred "source of strength" reading is allowable here, the use of *under* appears to accept the hierarchical view of the head over the members of the "body of Christ." The EWC statement could thus unintentionally imply acceptance of headship as authority.

The second feminist point made in this paragraph lies in the reference to the Holy Spirit, a reference that accomplishes two things. First, it completes the expected reference to the three members of the Trinity. Second, it calls to mind the function of the Holy Spirit to impel individual Christians to action, especially within the Christian community, and often within the context of worship—a sphere currently almost entirely under male control. An important part of this schema, and a common reason for invoking the Holy Spirit, is the strong evangelical belief that God may, through the Holy Spirit, command Christians to do things that are forbidden by human authorities.

The reference to the Holy Spirit is carried through in the reference to *exercis[ing] gifts*. Gifts are special talents or abilities, such as evangelism, teaching, pastoring (sometimes thought of as more or less equivalent to lay counselling), administration, and so on, to be used for the benefit of the church. They are distinct from secular or natural talents. The Holy Spirit presides over the conferring of some gift on each Christian, as well as over its exercise. Christians are expected to put some effort into finding their individual gifts and identifying appropriate outlets for them.

This entire segment conveys both orthodoxy, through its use of language, and a subtle warning to traditionalists, through the reference to the Holy Spirit, not to interfere with women's active participation in the church and Christian community. Indeed, it identifies the Holy Spirit as the source of women's freedom to operate outside of traditional bounds.

We come now to the most difficult portion of the paragraph, and perhaps of the entire statement: the use of *freed* instead of the more common *free*. *Freed* is normally used of a change from non-Christian to Christian status: one is "freed from sin" or "freed from the fear of judgment". The notion of being "freed to exercise gifts," however, is peculiar within evangelical orthodoxy; it cannot refer to conversion, since the gifts are not acquired until after conversion. It is entirely appropriate here, however, since the writers really do want to suggest that male dominance is one of the things that Christianity should free a person from. As in Paragraph 2, male dominance is presented as a facet of sin. There is also a suggestion that conversion is not complete until one accepts equality, and indeed the pattern of recognizing one's unacceptable state, converting, and becoming free works for both the original conversion and the "conversion" to feminism. (Certainly, many evangelical feminists were traditional evangelicals before they were feminists, and so this "second conversion" is entirely reasonable, and for many a recognizable pattern, given their own experience in the church.) Still, because of the careful phrasing, there is nothing that traditionalists could argue with, although they would certainly be aware that something was going on.

This distinction between *free* and *freed* is not unfamiliar to evangelicals. Indeed, because of the history of most conservative denominations, many evangelicals have readily available to them the notion of being freed by the Holy Spirit from adherence to more traditional religious forms ("the traditions of men"). Here the notion is turned around, so that standard evangelicalism becomes the oppressive tradition and "conversion" to feminism the God-inspired freeing.

The term *responsibly* appears to be addressed to all readers: to men as a warning that they are not exercising their own gifts responsibly if they prohibit others from exercising theirs; to women as a warning that, while traditional limitations may be lifted, women's behavior, like men's, must still be under the control of the Holy Spirit; and to traditionalists as a sort of reassurance that they need not fear for their churches, for the feminists are also concerned to do God's will.

PARAGRAPH 6:

We believe that the Bible which bears witness to Christ is the Word of God inspired by the Holy Spirit, and is the infallible guide and final authority for Christian faith and life.

PARAGRAPH 7:

We believe the church is the community of women and men who have been divinely called to fellowship with God and one another to seek and do God's will, looking forward to God's coming glorious kingdom.

These two paragraphs are fully orthodox. The phrase *to seek and do God's will* is arguably another point for feminism, since it brings to attention the accepted view that Christians have a duty to do God's will, again recalling the mandate to stand up for the truth despite opposition. Suggesting that God's will is not always obvious, but must be "sought," leaves room for non-traditional readings, since the traditional reading of any text is always the "obvious" one precisely because of its familiarity.

These two phrases are more than balanced by a series of formulas the very use of which affirms the writers' orthodoxy: *bears witness to Christ, infallible guide and final authority for Christian faith and life, fellowship with God, seek and do* (in its phrasing), *God's coming glorious kingdom.*

* * * * * *

What we have seen, then, is a statement of faith that mingles standard evangelical terminology and phrasings with alternate forms typical of the evangelical feminist movement. There are far more traditional terms, however, and many of the alternate forms are nothing more than an application of traditional terminology, with different emphasis, or with normally accompanying material deleted.

The structure of presentation is of interest as well, as noted earlier. The creedal statement starts with an entirely orthodox paragraph, introduces a significant amount of feminist terminology in paragraph 2, reverts almost entirely to orthodox terminology in paragraphs 3 and 4, and concentrates a series of overtly feminist points in paragraph 5. After this, however, we are back on orthodox ground again for the two closing paragraphs. It is no surprise that the main points of the statement are located in paragraphs 2 and 5, which are just those areas where feminists differ importantly from traditionalists.

This structure, in which radical ideas are doubly buffered, first by couching them in traditional terms, and second by placing them between traditionally accepted tenets, allows the writers to make clear their beliefs without giving a toehold for objection by traditionalists, who are an important part of the audience for this text. The fact that this can be done—that feminist positions *can* be stated in such a way that they anticipate and preclude traditionalist objections—reflects a curious paradox in traditional evangelical Christianity. The positions taken by the EWC in this statement are, as stated, within the range of acceptable evangelical doctrines, but, in their baldest form and presented as a unit, they would carry certain emotional overtones which would make them unacceptable to traditionalists. It is therefore necessary for the writers to separate the points they want to make and to establish their own *ethos* as competent Christians in order for their arguments to receive a hearing.

Ultimately, the text accomplishes two tasks required of ritual creedal statements. It "censors the EWC in," in Hoffman's terms, by reflecting the evangelical approach of the EWC, and so signals that organization's willingness to be "in fellowship with" any other orthodox evangelical organization. At the same time, however, it identifies itself as clearly feminist in its biblical interpretation.

That second function, the "censoring out" is of particular interest, for while an organization may normally choose how to emphasize or de-emphasize those features by which it distinguishes itself from other evangelical organizations, the EWC has had many of those choices made for it at the outset. As long as the statement was aimed at evangelicals, it was simply not possible to avoid the word *headship*, for example, in dealing with the structure of male-female relationships. And, on the other hand, once the necessary concepts had been incorporated into the statement, *with the appropriate terminology*, the statement could fulfill its ritual function of presenting the EWC as an organization properly within the evangelical "fellowship." This is not to say that all evangelicals would be obliged to agree with the statement. Rather, disagreement must proceed from within the group: the EWC could be criticized or ignored, but it could not be dismissed, as *Uplook* (as noted earlier) dismissed the Christians for Biblical Equality.

The ritual functions of the creedal statement, then, operate on two levels. First, the very existence of the statement constitutes a formal presentation of the organization to the evangelical community—a presentation validated by the ritually proper affirmations on required topics: the nature of the Deity, the place of humans in the universe, the Fall, redemption, the function of the Church, and so on. Within that context, the choice of ritually sanctioned linguistic forms establishes the authors, and so the organization, as worthy of a hearing. It is the difference between having a passport which identifies one as a citizen of a particular place, and being fluent in the language and customs of its denizens.

In this particular case, we can see what happened when the EWC changed its focus away from the evangelical community, for in 1990 the organization, after some internal soul-searching, changed its name to Evangelical & Ecumenical Women's Caucus (EEWC), and added to its agenda some issues, most notably support for lesbian and gay rights, that caused an exodus of its more conservative members. Many of those who left joined a new organization called Christians for Biblical Equality, which, while feminist in approach, retains a strongly evangelical focus and a conservative approach to hermeneutics.

The new EEWC statement of faith (see appendix) shows some change in the propositions presented; indeed, the changes in language are glaring. While the new statement of faith does not contradict any tenets of evangelical belief, it no longer reflects an organization of people fluent in the ritually prescribed presentation of evangelical Christian faith.

The EEWC Statement of Faith (1992)

We believe God is the Creator, Redeemer, and Sustainer of all.

We believe God created all people, female and male, in the divine image for relationship with God and one another.

We further believe our relationship with God was shattered by sin with a consequent disruption of all other relationships.

We believe God in love has made possible a new beginning through the incarnation in the life, death, and resurrection of Jesus Christ, who was and is truly divine and truly human.

We believe the Bible is the Word of God, inspired by the Holy Spirit, and is a central guide and final authority for Christian faith and life.

We believe the church is the community of women and men who have been divinely called to do God's will, exercising their gifts responsibly in church, home, and society, and looking forward to God's new creation.

Notes

1. I am indebted to Kevin Dungey, Charles Coleman, Sheila Webster Boneham, and Lesley Northup for extensive comments on earlier drafts. Responsibility for any errors in this paper is mine alone.

2. Marjorie Procter-Smith, *In Her Own Rite: Constructing Feminist Liturgical Tradition* (Nashville: Abingdon Press, 1990) 61.

3. Philip Schaff, *The Creeds of Christendom*, vol. 1: *The History of Creeds* (Grand Rapids, MI: Baker Book House, 1919); see also Stephen A. Hayes, "Worship and the New Canadian Statement of Faith," *Reformed Liturgy and Music* 19 (Spring 1985) 93-96; E. Glenn Hinson, "Creeds and Christian Unity: A Southern Baptist Perspective," *Journal of Ecumenical Studies* 23:1 (Winter 1986): 25-36; Robin A. Leaver, The Augsburg Confession and the Confessional Principle," *Churchman: Journal of Anglican Theology* 94:4 (1980): 345-352.

4. *Christianity Today* Editors, "The Christianity Today-Gallup Pole: An Overview," *Christianity Today* (December 1979): 12.

5. William J. Samarin, "Religious Motives in Religious Movements," *Internationales Jahrbuch für Religionsoziologie* 8 (1973): 163-174; Ruth Ann Borker, *Presenting the Gospel: Religious Communication and Expressive Strategies in Three Evangelical Churches in Edinburgh, Scotland*. Dissertation. University of California, Berkeley, 1974.

6. Carma van Liere, *Hallowed Fire: Faith Motivation of Early Women Activists* (Valley Forge, PA: Judson Press, 1991) 47ff.

7. Reprinted in Liere, *Hallowed Fire* 135-136.

8. EEWC Brochure; Liere, *Hallowed Fire* 97.

9. Linda Coleman, "The Language of 'Born-Again' Christianity," in *Proceedings of the Sixth Annual Meeting of the Berkeley Linguistics Society*, ed. Bruce Caron and others (Berkeley, CA: Berkeley Linguistics Society, 1980) 133-142.

10. A pattern of religious language use specialized to the degree that it amounts to a "technical jargon" is not unique to evangelicals, nor to English. To take one of many examples which could be cited, the advent of a Roman Catholic presence among the Dinka of the Sudan created a situation in which ordinary Dinka terms developed secondary, "technical" meanings specific to Christian theology, while retaining in other contexts their original Dinka meanings; see Godfrey Lienhardt, "The Dinka and Catholicism," in *Religious Organization and Religious Experience*, ed. J. Davis (London: Academic Press, 1982) 81-95.

11. See George Lakoff and Mark Johnson, *Metaphors We Live By* (Chicago: University of Chicago Press, 1980).

12. Jeff Mobley, quoted in Gustav Niebuhr, "Some Baptists Rejoin Democrats' Fold," *The Washington Post* (October 28, 1992): A1.

13. *Uplook* Editors, "Frontlines," *Uplook* (July-August 1992): 6.

14. Lawrence A. Hoffman, *Beyond the Text: A Holistic Approach to Liturgy* (Bloomington: Indiana University Press, 1989) 158.

15. J.N.D. Kelly, tr., *Rufinus: A Commentary on the Apostles' Creed* (Westminster, MD: Newman Press, 1955) 30; see also E. Glenn Hinson: "Confessions or Creeds in Early Christian Tradition," *Review and Expositor: A Baptist Theological Journal* 76 (Winter 1979): 5-16; Jean Pierre van Noppen, "Fides Quaerens Verbum Hodiernum: Alternative Creeds and Speech Acts," in *Language in Religion*, ed. Humphrey Tonkin and Allison Armstrong Keef (Lanham, MD: University Press of America, 1989) 70.

16. See, for example, Hinson, "Creeds and Christian Unity"; also F.G. Healey, "Creeds and Confessions of Faith," in *What Theologians Do*, ed. F.G. Healey (Grand Rapids, MI: Eerdmans, 1970) 141.

17. The statement is presented with the title "Statement of Faith". The paragraph numbering does not appear in the original, but is added here for the reader's convenience.

18. Here and throughout, quotations from the Bible are in the King James Version.

19. Nancy Hardesty, *Inclusive Language in the Church* (Atlanta: John Knox Press, 1987) 50.

20. See, for example, Gilbert Bilzekian, *Beyond Sex Roles: A Guide for the Study of Female Roles in the Bible* (Grand Rapids, MI: Baker Book House, 1985).

9

Bodyworship:
The Gender-Masquerade
of Fashion, Beauty, and Style

Kathryn Allen Rabuzzi

WHEN I WAS A LITTLE GIRL, I REMEMBER HEARING THE APHORISM, "Water, water, everywhere, but not a drop to drink." I have no idea why I learned it or what it was intended to teach me in those days before the prevalence of water pollution was widely known. But I keep remembering it nowadays in slightly altered form: Body, body, everywhere but not . . . In this age of AIDS, when bodies have become in some sense untouchable and out of reach, it seems a curious paradox that everywhere we hear about body. Academic books and papers sometimes seem to talk of nothing else. Nearly every magazine is full of bodies and body parts. Almost everyone works out or at least talks about the shape their bodies are in. And many mainstream individuals nowadays variously pierce, tatoo, or otherwise mutilate their bodies. What does all this mean?

I would suggest that it means that the cliché "bodyworship" has become reinvested with a very powerful, literal meaning. We now worship the body not just in the superficial way once connected with that phrase, but in the much deeper, religious sense that the word "worship" originally meant. Major aspects of this worship include the iconography, clothing, and adornment with which we variously understand, cover, and highlight that body and the diverse treatments to which we subject it.

Whereas many feminists are quick to criticize such body attention in women (Naomi Schorr's 1992 bestseller *The Beauty Myth* is illustrative), negative analysis of women's beauty rituals does not cover the entire picture. Body adornment, fashion, and the like are not always simple responses to male desires and commercial greed. They also reflect important ritual enactments for some women (as well as some male transvestites) of a sort which connects directly to religious practices.

Consider, for instance, the ritual properties of dress, which have a long and ancient history within many traditions both east and west. Such dress may be as simple as the distinguishing round white clerical collars of Christian clergy, the saffron robes of Buddhist monks, or the plain clothing of Hindu priests. Conversely, ritual dress may be as elaborate as the full regalia of the pope, the kimono, outer coat, and black lacquered silk hat of the Shinto clergy, or the personally crafted bird and animal masks and garments of Siberian shamans. Whereas ritual dress is often restricted to priestly figures, in some traditions—such as Orthodox Judaism—all male members dress in prayer shawl, phylacteries, and skullcap.

Often ritualized dress varies according to gender, so that historically, in many Christian traditions and particularly in Roman Catholicism, women were required to cover their heads, men to bare theirs; conversely, in Judaism men are still required to cover theirs and women, who formerly did not, are increasingly doing so as well. Common to many traditions are elements of transvestism, as seen in the dress-like robes worn by male priests in traditions as diverse as Roman Catholicism, Shintoism, and Taoism. Even more overtly, genderbending is the practice of North American shamans known as *berdaches* who typically lived as "wives" to other men as well as engaging in crossdressing, such cross-gender practices being considered signs of sacrality in many traditions. What unites the enormous diversity of ritual dress is an underlying belief that special dress relates somehow to special power or powers.

The term "ritual" may be problematic for some readers. This is understandable because "ritual" is hotly contested nowadays among academics. Probably one of the best, if not necessarily the most illuminating, definitions comes from religionist Catherine Bell, who prefers the term *ritualization*.

> Ritualization always aligns one within a series of relationships linked to the ultimate sources of power. Whether ritual empowers or disempowers one in some practical sense, it always suggests the ultimate coherence of a cosmos in which one takes a particular place.[1]

In our own contemporary postmodern culture, the "embodied" world of fashion provides an excellent example of a venue in which ritualized dress and behavior give many women a place which they can stake out as their own, thereby creating a cosmos which coheres for them. What then, is the nature of this cosmos?

* * * * * *

Warning: The scenes that follow may be offensive to some sensibilities.

Scene I. It is 10:30 on a sunny Saturday morning in 1991. I sit, mini-blinds drawn, in our television room, sorting laundry, listening, but only half-watching CNN. "Good morning," comes the anticipated voice, and I sit up. "Welcome to the World of Beauty, Fashion, and Style. This is your host, Elsa Klensch." I sit, mesmerized, for the next half hour, as Klensch takes me through a preview of the Spring Collections, highlighting the venerable Geoffrey Beene, the sexy Georgio Armani, and the bad boy Isaac Mizrahi. After a short break, we view some stunning jewelry creations by Paloma Picasso. After another break, we enter the fabulous twenty-five room, Sixteenth Arrondissement apartment of the Countess Jacqueline de Ribes, with its Louis 16th furniture and museum-like bibelots. A brief glimpse at the formerly *outre*, now comparatively restrained, fashions of Kenzo follows, and then the familiar voice purrs, over the fashion music beat and brief preview of next week's show, ". . . and that's all for this week's edition of Beauty, Fashion, Style by Elsa Klensch."

No, what I have just presented to you is not, as some may have wished or feared, some steamy back-room leather bar scene. But within the currently permissible bounds of what is "seemly" for academic thinking and discourse, my spectacle is nonetheless highly suspect on several grounds. The scene is certainly not recognizably feminist, and it *is* unmistakably materialistic; it also strongly suggests narcissism; some may consider it superficial. In short, this scene represents a kind of forbidden fruit.

Scene II. It is a late August day, around 6:30 P.M., sometime in the late 1970s. I am walking, wearing jeans and a silk shirt. Approximately half of my normal three-mile route is dotted with houses, the other half being open pasture land. I am deep in thought, planning an article, but not so lost that I don't hear the sound of an approaching car, nor the slowing of its motor. I turn. The approaching car is bright orange, its driver extremely young. For a moment I mistake him for one of my spring semester's students.

"How ya doin?" he asks.

I am puzzled. It's not my student; it's nobody I know. Why would so young a man be asking *me* . . .? Just then he speeds up, pulls into a driveway, turns around, and goes back the way he came. I smile to myself, figuring that he must have seen me from the back, presumed from my jeans that I was "young," and had begun his opening gambit before he fully realized I was not.

I walk on. The mile passes quickly as I wrestle with possible topic arrangements for my paper. Maybe I won't take my full walk this evening. It's plenty light out, but I don't know. I just have a funny feeling. At the end of the road there's a sort of lovers' lane. And I'm not quite sure, but even in my revery I think I may have seen a streak of orange pull in there. Probably just my imagination, but who knows? I don't feel like being hassled. I'll just take a longer walk tomorrow.

Just past the last house on the road, across from an open field full of high grass, I turn. I am smiling to myself: I've just figured out . . . I hear footsteps, running. Damn. Why can't that guy leave me along? Damn, damn, damn. Now I'll lose my train of thought. I am not at all afraid. The steps slow. I turn. It is the same young man, now in step right beside me.

Irritated, I ask: "What are you doing?"

"What do you mean? I'm just walking."

All of a sudden I am afraid. Politeness be damned, I start to run. Without warning, I find myself down in the middle of the road. I think "Oh my God, I'm in the middle of the road. If a car comes, I'll be run over."

* * * * * *

I'm one of the fortunate ones—I did not get raped—all I was left with were a few bad bruises, some bad fright, a trip to the police station, *and* a comment from my neighbor, a woman, who said, "You *did* look awfully appealing in your jeans and silk shirt, you know."

By now, in the wake of the Anita Hill–Clarence Thomas circus and the William Kennedy Smith and Mike Tyson trials, this particular issue is surely no longer alien territory to any adult in America. Regardless of who may or may not have been telling the truth in any of those situations, the issues raised by each case are significant in a number of ways—ethically, legally, psychologically, and so forth. They are also extremely important from a religious perspective, although not just in the way the word "religion" might automatically seem to suggest. With my two diverse scenes as backdrop, I want to explore the world of fashion, style, and beauty dramatized by my opening scene. That world is clearly something far more than just a clever mix of superficiality and narcissism. Or a world whose primary purpose is to make women desirable sex objects for men. Rather, this is a world that thrives because it possesses a very special kind of power. It is a power that enables those who enter the world of fashion, beauty, and style to ritually employ icons and engage in body enactments that satisfy deep human needs no longer served by the most formalized religions.

Although this claim may seem extreme, even blasphemous to some, consider some of the similarities between the worlds of fashion and religion. The fashion world is first of all a world which, like that created in a pre-Vatican II Mass, for example, stimulates almost all the senses. Sight, of course, is absolutely primary, this being a spectacle *par excellence*, with "viewings" of clothes and people-watching both *sine qua nons*. But the kinetic sense runs a very close second, for this is also a world in which both models and their imitators—that is, the watching, would-be consumers—are encouraged to move, to "enact," as it were, their bodies, by means of different styles and textures of clothing. Part of the spectacle's appeal rests on the fluidity or molding quality of the clothes as they variously move with or cling to their wearer's body. And of course it is ultimately the bodies themselves that matter most in this secular religion wherein salvation of the soul has been replaced by salvation of the body.

The tactile sense is also strongly appealed to, with contrasting textures, shiny silk charmeuse, for instance, juxtaposed with rough Harris tweed, compelling the participant to reach out and feel, not only with her fingers, but also to anticipate the feel of the clothes against her own body. Less immediately obvious, perhaps, is the appeal to the thermal sense—how cozily that coat envelopes the model's body, how temptingly that dress, with its strategically placed openings, provides spaces cool to the skin, and so forth.

Somewhat less directly, sound too, although obviously not inherent in the clothes *per se*, is, as background music, an indispensable part of their secular appeal. Who, anymore, can imagine a fashion show without the beat of rock, rap, or disco? Its absence would, if anything, be even more striking than the lack of singing or chanting in a traditional religious ceremony. Also closely aligned to this powerful world of fashion, beauty, and style, although not overt in a taped fashion show, is its olfactory appeal. The entire realm of perfumes, lotions, creams, and such assorted unguents, makes a powerful statement all its own. Of the most commonly recognized senses, then, taste alone is omitted, a situation similar to that encountered in most church services, although present in many other religious rituals. In this regard, the ancillary world of spa cuisine may be said to play a role not unlike that of various ritualized religious meals.

Other elements from the world of beauty, fashion, and style that strongly suggest a parallel with traditional religions include its heavy emphasis on doctrine. Fashion "bibles" abound, ranging from the gossipy weekly "W to the trade-oriented *Women's Wear Daily*, and from such teen-targeted magazines as *Sassy* to the "mature" *Mirabella* with a whole raft of more generalized offerings in between such as *Vogue*, *Elle*, and *Bazaar*. Cassettes and books too numerous to count cover every possible aspect of creating and maintaining a body beautiful.

Most cogent of all, however, is the way this world functions to create for its adherents a sense of "salvation." This is a salvation geared to those who experience little or no presence of what some call "God," that is, a transcendent spiritual force, and who harbor no expectation of life after death, and who make no particular separation of body and soul or psyche. For individuals who feel that body and self are equivalent, that the here and now is all there is, the world of fashion, beauty, and style offers up a fair approximation of religious ritual. Especially suggestive, in this regard, is the bodywork of exercise guru Richard Simmons, who "saves" the obese in a kind of 12-step program.

Yet while this powerful world of beauty, fashion, and style can provide great personal satisfaction to its adherents, as my second scene implies, it is also a potentially threatening world for numerous reasons. One of the most important is that, given the kind of secular culture now shared on a worldwide basis by the global village predicted by Marshall McLuhan back in the early 1960s, spectacles of body-display—whether embodied, as here, in a fashion show, or by other rituals presented by video, television, film or live show—not only can enhance, they also can destroy the selfhood of those who watch. And the nature of this challenge is intensifying now that we are rapidly becoming a world in which virtual reality comes into its own commercially. In that nearly possible brave new world of reality-altering images, the icons and rituals of body-display promise to assume even greater power than they now have, as distinctions between external and internal "reality"— always tenuous at best—become further confused by the simulations of virtual reality. Yet for many people, an even greater threat comes from fashion in the way it so readily points up the relativistic nature of gender. Although I would argue that all fashion can be construed as "drag," that threat is most apparent in what is ordinarily called "doing drag."

Usually the term "drag" is primarily applied to gay males who put on women's clothes with the intention of looking like women—or even, paradoxically, looking *too much* like them— without, in fact, actually *becoming* women. In doing drag, a practitioner unleashes power because he or she is automatically enacting numerous variations on the split between an external stereotype and an internally-experienced self. And that split entails potential dangers. It allows a practitioner variously to "become" "someone else" for herself, for her beholders, or—more commonly—for a mix of both. But in all these cases the desired transformation is *not* entirely in the performer's control and will thus possibly turn out very differently from what she expects. For instance, a woman may want to be fashionable simply for herself, without regard to what others see and think. Similarly, a man may want to appear as a woman without being thought gay. But neither has control over the responses of beholders. Thus while being fashionable or doing drag both allow their respective practitioners to "pretend" to "be" something they are not, or feel they are not, very often just the opposite phenomenon is also simultaneously operative. Being fashionable or doing drag may also allow practitioners to "be" or "become" who they already are, rather than, or in addition to, someone alien. This duality, which is part of the appeal of masking, is a significant component of the dangerous part of fashion or drag.

A large part of this dangerous power also emerges in the way body enactment has a potential for confusing the expectations of others. In the case of the drag queen, the queen has the ability to so thoroughly mix up culturally accepted categories that both s\he and her viewers lose their bearings. Who or what is s\he? We all know this kind of confused-category-fear from childhood, when the masks and costumes of Halloween, far from delighting, terrified us; when Santa Claus sent us shrieking to our mother's arms; when the game of "Where's Kathy . . . I don't see Kathy . . . where did Kathy go?" goaded us into a frenzy of existential terror. This fearful experience places us at the very borders of non-existence.

Yet mixed with this fear is playfulness, for drag is by definition a playful art, that is, one that plays with the original categories that constitute it: maleness, femaleness, fashion, and spectacle. By the very act of donning what is conventionally accepted in contemporary western cultures as "female" dress, a man automatically questions assigned gender roles, even as he burlesques them. The play of doing drag also exists in the space created between the "self" externalized by the drag and the original self underlying it. Whether this "play" is itself "playful" depends upon the particular performer. In the case of someone who fails to understand the detachability of image and "self," for example, it is not. But for someone like Madonna, in her many well-publicized instances of doing drag, the enactment is clearly playful. This characteristic of "play" in both senses is absolutely critical to understanding the power of ritual enactment.

Equally important in the play of doing drag is the way it challenges notions of what constitutes fashion. After all, why *can't* a man wear a dress? Why *do* any of us wear what we wear? Why do so many of us accept the dictates of fashion and/or custom? Furthermore, the notion of spectacle is foregrounded in various ways as well. What is it we are seeing when we see a man dressed as a woman? What is the connection between dress and underlying body and underlying "core-self," assuming such an entity can any longer be said to exist? What is the relationship of the seen to the unseen and so forth? The play and interplay of all these elements of drag constitute a critical dimension of its power.

By no means is drag and the power underlying it limited simply to gay males, however. Women, too, particularly lesbians, speak of drag in reference to clothing choices which reflect their preferred gender roles, with words like "butch" and "femme." Furthermore, gay males often refer to the calculated dress of such gay movie idols as Marlene Dietrich and Judy Garland as drag. Fashion, in the sense of high fashion, thus readily assumes the status of drag—all drag being a kind of "trying on" of different "selves" by means of costuming the body in different ways.

From my own personal experience, for example, I know that much of my pleasure in shopping bears no relationship to whether I actually buy something or not. Instead, I enjoy trying on clothes I would never dream of actually wearing in public, much less buying, because in trying them on, I am in a sense, momentarily "becoming" a different self. I can become a wealthy socialite, assuming I have the nerve to try on a $1,000 outfit by Escada and Armani; a sleazy slut if I try on garments in Frederick's of Hollywood; or a WASPy Junior Leaguer if I slip on Talbot's dresses; and so on. I can even, if I do choose to buy, go out into the world beyond the changing booth and readily "pass" for the particular image I have chosen for that day. Here the power of the image is more tamed than in the case of the more flamboyant forms of transsexual drag. Yet here too, in the world of fashion, potential danger lurks. The danger here is that of losing one's selfhood by taking icons and body-enactments too seriously. A currently popular trend known as Image Consulting is illustrative.

Image Consulting is a practice which, like the extremely

popular seasonal color theory which preceded and now co-exists with it, is designed to help a woman realize who she is, primarily in an external, bodily sense. Based on a blend of body-type and personality, Image Consulting generally takes place in a small group conducted by individuals who presumably have been trained in spotting and applying a typology based on dramatic, romantic, classic, and gamine categories.

Here is my own eye-witness account. I went with two other women to a boutique in Camillus, New York, at a prearranged time on an August afternoon in 1991. Four other women, all strangers to us and to each other, were already there. The two boutique owners (this was a day on which their shop was traditionally closed) ushered us into the front room of the boutique where we gathered round a large table. After a brief orientation by one of the two boutique owners, each of us was handed a two-page style quiz. One woman at a time was then taken off to a far corner of the room for an appraisal by the two leaders while the rest of us filled out our style questionnaires. Questions directed us to indicate what look we would automatically choose in skirts, suit jackets, blouses, dresses, jewelry, and prints. To help us decide, illustrations of diverse styles were included. The last two questions were the most interesting. The first focused on the style-image the test-taker most favored, with choices including "Egyptian goddess," "1990's all-American athletic look," "1930's Park Avenue," "Gibson girl or gay 1890s," and "1920s." The second question asked, "Which category do you associate with?" Answers included "Majestic" (Katharine Hepburn, Lauren Bacall, Kathleen Turner); "Girl Next Door" (Candice Bergen, Chris Evert, Carol Burnett); "Aristocratic" (Grace Kelly, Diane Sawyer, Cybill Shepard); "Enchanting" (Elizabeth Taylor, Marilyn Monroe, Jaclyn Smith); and "Effervescent" (Audrey Hepburn, Mia Farrow, Leslie Caron).

The simultaneously occurring individual evaluations with the two boutique owners included appraisal of face shape by means of assorted cardboard shapes held up to the face to see if it was round, square, oval, rectangular, or heart-shaped; determination of body-structure; height; weight; and the like. After each woman's individual evaluation, each of us shared our answers to the style quiz; following this, the two leaders consulted before decreeing our respective types and giving us the booklet appropriate to them. The remainder of the three-and-a-half hour session was devoted to further refinements, with specific suggestions for creating our newly acquired self-images.

What struck me most about this entire procedure is not the content we were given, but the responses of the other women. Not one of them initially knew her own body type nor, more startling to me, her habitual clothing preferences. Furthermore, once they were told by the two leaders what type they were, each of them immediately pounced on that information as "gospel." One woman, for example, moaned that she had just placed a catalog order for some clothes that she now realized she should never have ordered because they did not fit her newly acquired image. She asked if she could bring in the catalog for help in selecting a totally different replacement order. Another woman, one of the two I came in with, told me several weeks later that she now feels guilty—her precise word—when she isn't wearing the kind of clothing or jewelry that her image "requires."

These responses disturb me. Here what we see, in contrast to the deliberate adoption of dress to display or provoke that is typical of drag queens, is just the reverse. Here are women whose self-awareness is so drastically limited that they have no sense that fashion and self-image both exist in a symbolic universe. They experienced Image Consulting literally as *the* way for them to be forever after. Not one of them appeared to realize that she was, in the process, relinquishing power to those she considered more expert on herself than she! Rather than *playing* with the images suggested to them, these women were allowing the assigned images to play with them, that is, they seemed willing to enthrall themselves to the images the so-called authorities declared fit them. This is very different from the willful, self-controlled manipulation of images typically found in the play of drag queens.

Some important questions emerge from exploring manipulation of images inherent in the worlds of fashion and drag. These include the following. If one is a "natural" image of something viewed as so desirable by a dominant culture that others seek to alter themselves to "become" that image, then what does that situation do to the selfhood of the originals? Of the imitators? And what is the relation of imitators to originals and vice versa?

Doubtless it is fitting that I try to answer some of these questions by choosing words taken directly from the world of beauty, fashion, and style. Fashion photographer Steven Meisel muses suggestively when he says:

> At the time I was growing up, fashion pictures were much more fantasy-oriented. It wasn't girls hailing cabs and stuff like that. They were romantic, glamorous, and tragic. I used the fantasy and glamour of those magazines as an escape mechanism. They drew me into a dream world. I don't think we have that sense of romance and glamour anymore, but I'd like to re-create it.[2]

Of the several words that stand out to me in this statement—romantic, glamour, fantasy, escape, and dream world—"fantasy" will have to stand for them all.

The word "fantasy" can be variously interpreted as escapist or transcendent. Either way it is potentially dangerous. From an escapist perspective, fantasy is to be avoided—it is something that shuts us off from a presumed "real" world to which we must learn to adapt in order to get on with our lives. Fantasy implies avoidance and escape rather than encounter and challenge. But that very same word—"fantasy"—can also suggest a world transformed or, depending on one's epistemology, formed, so that it becomes the very act of creation itself. It is this latter understanding of the word that seems most promising, given our postmodern problematic which assumes we do, in fact, create our own worlds, that no *a priori* or separate world can be said to exist. When used this way, fantasy is necessarily the vehicle by which we each bring into being the world we choose to inhabit. Far from being negative and avoidant, fantasy, understood this way, is the *sine qua non* of existence. Without it, no world exists.

Yet, such creation may as easily be demonic as divine. For example, in my own case, by enjoying both my blondness and my world of fashion, am I not complicitous in creating and maintaining a world of white-male-dominated values? And if some of those values are ones that I like, what does that mean? Is this purely and simply another example of false consciousness? Or is it possible and/or legitimate to take some of the images idealized by a sometimes despicable culture and use them as fantasy building blocks of one's own? Put another way, these questions boil down to one: will the real "I" please come forward? One problem with this formulation, however, is that given our postmodern ways of conceptualizing, this is a question so absurd—with its assumption that there is an "I" or a "me" to step forward—that it is nearly unaskable. Yet if no such thing as a "real" "I" can be said to exist, then, to borrow from a song popular in the 1960s—I no longer recall its title— we are left with yet another question: "Is that all there is?" with "that" referring variously to image, display, stereotype, and drag. And if the song question says it all, it means that the only power in the world resides in our images. If so, does that make us all idolaters? Or does it mean that, without realizing it, we have all, already, stepped into a virtual world?

Notes

1. Catherine Bell, *Ritual Theory, Ritual Practice* (New York and Oxford: Oxford University Press, 1992) 141.
2. *Advocate* (3 December 1991): 92.

10

Expanding the X-Axis: Women, Religious Ritual, and Culture

Lesley A. Northup

THE WORK OF PIONEER FEMINIST THEOLOGIANS LIKE ROSEMARY RAD-
ford Ruether, Carol Christ, Judith Plaskow, and Mary Daly established some time ago the truism that the western religious
tradition is, at its core, patriarchal. Its central "master image,"
to use Lawrence Hoffman's phrase,[1] is Rudolf Otto's *mysteri-
um tremendum et fascinans*.[2] God is "up there," "out there,"
"far-out." God is also irredeemably male. Western religious
ritual reflects and supports this master image: God is high; we
are low. Churches are ordered in hierarchical ladders of as-
cending power and authority; steepled houses of worship are
located on hilltops, at the *axis mundi*;[3] worshipers face raised
altars, with reredos that draw the eye ever higher; ritual pos-
tures involve variations of bowing, kneeling, and prostrating;
even immersion baptism sinks initiates below ground level in
order to raise them up again—literally and figuratively—
afterward.

Perhaps we could make an interesting case for some biological imperative that underlies this essentially male verticality—
men stand taller than women, male animals of the higher orders copulate upright, the erect penis thrusts upward. Regard-

less, this up-and-down, y-axis orientation is clearly identifiable—one need only listen to the imagery in Christian hymns, for example, to notice it immediately. Certainly, feminist critical thinkers recognized it quickly—and, for some time, tried to work within its confines.

In the wake of the feminist theological analysis of existing tradition, however, many have despaired of the repairability of the semitic traditions, and are now seeking not to reform western religion, but to abandon it, developing a unique and separate women's religious community. Thus, women like Daly are well beyond any semblance of lingering interest in the Christianity of their childhoods, and are exploring alternative forms of religiosity that may include the reclamation of goddess devotion, polytheism, or nontheistic spirituality with eastern or New Age accents.

But while feminist theology has focussed largely on the "top-down" intellectual challenge of identifying patriarchy and redefining traditional answers to the great questions of the nature of the divine and of our relationship with it—or, of late, on providing alternative models for spirituality—it has been less concerned with what could be called the "bottom-up" hermeneutical task of examining praxis to uncover meaning. That is, we still need to take a good, hard look at what real people are really doing in their religious ritualization—not just what ideal people are ideally doing—and what that means (in this regard, the feminist critique of secular life is ahead of the theological critique). If, in fact, ritual precedes theology and even myth, as many scholars today would agree, ritual praxis is the key to understanding religiosity. Too often, we have underestimated the importance of ritual as a crucial analytical category. But, as ritualist Catherine Bell points out, ritual is "powerful not only in the shaping of a social ethos, but also in the articulation, redefinition, and legitimation of cultural realities."[4]

Examining the way ritual affects and is affected by women reveals that distinctive gender-based ritual patterns occur regularly in Western religion. These include traditional gender-defined ceremonial elements, such as the spatial separation of men and women in an orthodox synagogue,[5] or the sex-segregated foot washing central to Seventh-Day Adventism.[6] They reflect problems of inclusivity in ritual language. They also surface in arguments over the ordination of women to roles of church leadership, and differences in how those roles are enacted when they are filled by women. And they ultimately issue forth in the proliferation of new and/or reclaimed religious rituals designed specifically by and for women.

New scholarship on women's rituals (both from within and outside of the tradition) has dealt almost exclusively with the latter. As long ago as 1985, Ruether wrote an outline of what she called—and many other women are now calling—women-church, discussing rituals appropriate to women's spirituality within the Christian tradition.[7] That movement has grown significantly; indeed, there are now even national women-church conferences. As Ruether puts it: "Women have begun to take the shaping of the symbolic universe of meaning into their own hands."[8] More recently, Diane Neu of WATER,[9] among others, has authored several volumes of women-church liturgies. Janet Walton and Marjorie Proctor-Smith have just published an anthology of feminist liturgies; and Barbara G. Walker has published *Women's Rituals: A Sourcebook*, meant as a non-scholarly, popular guide for "the sort of women who have thought about starting a spirituality group, but can't imagine what kind of activities such a group might engage in."[10]

Missing from this literature, however, is any systematic examination of the way women actually ritualize—not just the way they *should*. There is still a substantial hermeneutical task here that goes beyond merely reclaiming ancient practices or suggesting appropriate symbols. We need to uncover the meaning inherent in women's rituals, as they are practiced both in new spirituality groups and in more familiar settings.

Perhaps it would be useful to take a look at what constitutes women's rituals. Walker's book gives a fascinating glimpse of some ritual elements that can be considered particularly appropriate to women's spirituality, even if, as Walker writes, "you don't believe in anything at all." Some of her suggestions may sound hilarious to orthodox ears: in the "zoo game," for instance, a woman impersonates a chosen animal, right down to the donkey ears or cottontail. In "Copycats," women play a version of "Simon Says," and are encouraged, among other things, to "Stamp. Giggle. Scream . . . Kick the wall. Smell a flower . . . Take off a garment. . . Perform a bump and grind . . .

Moan. Purr. . . . Play dead. Crawl. . . [or] Reenact an embarrass-
ing moment,"[11] of which this would certainly be one, for most
people.

While these are intended to be somewhat playful rituals,
others are intensely serious, and rituals of play are balanced
against those of healing, learning, initiating, passaging, and so
on. Women ritualizing touch, dance, sing, keep silence, share,
and create. They use as symbols elemental earth, fire, and water; crafted quilts, weavings, and art; ancient stones, plants,
and runes; personal objects, stories, and relationships.

But almost all women's rituals share a distinctive quality—
they are horizontally oriented. Women ritualizing sit in circles,
not in rows; women use earth in their rituals, not just those
things that rise up out of it; women move laterally in religious
dance, not only forward in formal procession; women construct sacred space by redistributing a heap of stones horizontally, not piling stones higher and higher until they form sky-
scraping cathedrals. Both new and old women's rituals—as rituals—stand in direct contradistinction to the verticality inherent in patriarchal religion. Indeed, women ritualize in patterns
that emphasize not the power structures mapped along the y-
axis, but the communities spreading on the x-axis. This is perhaps not a new observation, but its application to the critical
category of ritual practice has not yet been clearly drawn.[12]

The hermeneutical question impels us to ask what all this
means. As Ruether says: "One needs not only to engage in rational theoretical discourse about this journey; one also needs
deep symbols and symbolic actions to guide and interpret the
actual experience of the journey."[13] More than that, however,
we also need some clear interpretive framework for all this
new symbol appropriation. It is clear that, as the various authors of these rituals intended, they are in keeping with deep,
mythical "master images" that are definitely not Ottonian.
Their focus is not on transcendence, but on community, memory, sharing, imagination, oral narrative, nature. These are
horizontal categories—they reach out across space and time,
not beyond it; they celebrate human, not divine, experience;
they emphasize process, not completion; they connect with the
earth, not the sky; they encourage relationship, not distance.

The inherent horizontality of religious ritual experienced
by, developed by, and reclaimed by women frees it from the

bonds of verticality; it neither vanishes unreachably in the ether of an infinitely high transcendence, nor ends with a thud at ground level. Rather, it spreads out. And in spreading, it reaches beyond the small community where it originates, beyond the larger religious organization surrounding that community, beyond religious applications at all.[14]

Indeed, this expansion along the x-axis leads to a significant crossover between women's ritualization and the wider, secular culture—the very crossover the vertically oriented semitic religions have tried so assiduously to avoid. This propensity to expand outward has blurred the distinction between religion and culture, with two practical consequences. The first is that it has contributed to the growing gulf between traditional and modernist believers. Hoffman, a rabbi whose specialization is liturgics, contends that Ottonian language and imagery is being inexorably displaced by a new "master image" of community in a changing culture that no longer understands the vocabulary of transcendence. Traditionalists generally attack this development as a dilution of the true faith, and try to maintain a clear boundary between the holy and the secular. As one church publication moaned: "For many . . . today a celebration of the Eucharist seems more concerned with the realization of the Church as a community and as a family than with the stupendous . . . worship of a God who in every Mass comes to dwell sacramentally among us."[15] Some—including many women—would find this a laudable advance, not a danger.

Fundamentalists and other conservatives are struggling to keep issues that affect women directly—such as abortion or birth control—within the purview of religious law and standards, which are believed to have distinct and unbridgeable boundaries, while women—often very religious ones—claim these as cultural, social, and legal issues. Conversely, women are bringing into the churches rituals for occasions formerly considered properly in the secular realm—services of healing for rape or abuse, divorce rites, adoption ceremonies.

The second consequence, as mentioned, is that this x-axis expansion has allowed women to sidle away from the churches of their upbringings in order to pursue alternative forms of spirituality. Those women interested in new women's spiritual groups have felt themselves freed from any "feeling of absolute dependence" on a transcendent God. In these settings, the divine is much more accessible at ground level; the deity, if one is supposed at all, is sympathetic and approachable—the goddess, or ancestors, or helpful spirits. Often, the divine is posited as the latent energy or strength in each woman and in the community, ideas that echo with the vedantic and Buddhist resonances of our age. In either case, the divine as imaged by women seems no longer to demand abject surrender, except in the sense that we all must surrender to the natural ebb and flow of life; women's rituals are freed from visual, spatial, temporal, experiential, and ethical commitment to vertical imagery and theology.

This freedom to ritualize—and symbolize—horizontally leads to a positive and healthy interchange with culture, no longer perceived by women as the enemy—"secular humanism." When women are ritualizing, religion and culture are perceived as cooperative, conjoined, inseparable, part of an integrated whole. There is little concern with protecting the precincts of the holy. Consequently, women may be freer to perceive the holiness of everyday living and human relationship, and to incorporate them into a religious worldview. For feminists, this means integrating issues of politics and justice with ritual; for more traditional women, it may mean an increased need for inclusivity or a call to church leadership or a greater commitment to social outreach.

Moreover, feminist theology and ritual theory have aggressively incorporated culture into spirituality. Take, for example, the figurative and literal quilt so eloquently discussed by Diann Neu.[16] The image of the quilt is not used accidentally by women. A quilt is homespun, created, flat, horizontal, spreading, secular, narrative. It draws in, it includes, it comforts, it represents, it remembers. It crosses over what patriarchal religions perceive as an inherent boundary between believers' mundane behavior and their expected religious behavior—a boundary that women constantly traverse, without noticing.

This blurring of religious and cultural lines stemming from the groundedness of women's rituals has deeper roots and is historically less deliberate than the conscious connection drawn today by feminist ritualizers. Indeed, in many ways feminist ritual theology builds upon this preexisting—but relatively unexamined—reality.

Examples abound, not only from the twentieth century, but from earlier periods. Consider, for instance, Karen Sue Hybertsen's work on the role of women in traditional Halloween celebrations.[17] In origin, Halloween was clearly a religious observation focussed principally on communication with—or, conversely, avoidance of—spirits. Halloween celebrations, however, evolved largely in the late Victorian period, during which they became a domestic communal festivity presided over almost exclusively by women. Periodicals and books of the period gave plenty of advice to hostesses on how to incorporate ancient rituals and divination games into a community-building house party with mystery and fun. Religious observance and everyday Victorian domesticity merged indistinguishably. Again, when women are doing the ritualizing, religion and culture overlap comfortably.

Other examples, some more obvious than others, suggest themselves. Consider the evolution of ritualized forms of address for clergy. In the Anglican tradition, which has the most heartburn over this question, ordained men could comfortably be called "Father." When ordination was extended to women, the question, "What do you call a woman priest?" was never resolved. Men who liked the parental-authority image of fatherhood thought it would be a good idea to call women clergy "Mother," though this had some obvious problems. Women's response to the question—and it *is* a ritual problem, not just a technical one—has largely been to opt for the unclerical and informal use of first names over any distinctive title at all. While this is by no means a universal phenomenon, an extensive survey I concluded recently indicated that it is the most common option.[18] Again, there seems to be a natural evolution here to more commonly accepted cultural norms, rather than distinctively religious or hierarchical ones, when women are doing the choosing.

Women's ritualization does not always tug in the direction of greater secularity. For example, we could mention the evolution of Kwanzaa, the African-American winter holiday. It is true that this case is more complex, since Kwanzaa began in 1966 at the instigation of a Black man—Maulana Karenga—and has been largely organized and popularized by men; this is to be expected in a culture in which religious leadership is predominantly male and heavily authoritarian.

But the rituals of Kwanzaa are hearth rituals—domestic, family-oriented, and clearly female in both origin and execution; as actually practiced, Kwanzaa is in style and content very much a women's ritual. Kwanzaa was originally conceived as a secular and cultural alternative to Christmas, but now is understood as a complementary ritual, largely because so many African-American women were unwilling to abandon their religious roots in favor of a purely cultural celebration. As Kwanzaa is now celebrated, there are elements of both African tribal religion and Western Christianity, as well as African culture. Again, in this case, women's influence has blurred the traditional religion/culture boundary; indeed, it would seem that women are most comfortable ritually in a sort of liminal space that overarches the two categories—that the blurred area is itself the place of truest resonance for women's ritualization.[19]

While most of these observations have reflected the situation in the United States, they may well hold true elsewhere, at least in the Americas. For example, consider the growing cult of Santeria, until recently an underground phenomenon, but now in the legal limelight in Miami, where the large Cuban population keeps it very much alive. Santeria is a religion heavily dominated by women (despite the implicit superiority of the *babalao* to the *babalocha*). Many of the rituals involve home, family, body, divination, food preparation—in short, horizontal, female concerns and influences. In the cognate Afro-Brazilian religions, women are clearly in charge; they are both the temple leaders and chief devotees, as well as the diviners.[20] And even though a principal ritual element in both these forms of Afro-Christian belief is the "mounting" of believers by their *orishas*, or saints, these deities do not descend like Jesus onto the altar, but are properly earthbound. Here again, religion—actually two of them, Roman Catholicism and Yoruba beliefs—is conjoined with and almost indistinguishable from Caribbean culture and a whole way of life in a comingling several centuries old.

In summary, then, women ritualize horizontally—communally, bodily, earthily—rather than vertically and transcendently, and this is reflected in and generated by their ritual symbols and behaviors. Moreover, women's ritualization appears to expand outward from the narrower religious sphere into the larger context of culture, melding the two realms into a fairly agreeable alliance that has proven to be a comfortable medium for women's spirituality. This stands in fairly clear contradistinction to the more vertical and hierarchical ritual models available in traditional religious systems usually dominated by men.

This has interesting implications not only for feminists and women's studies scholars, but for theologians, religionists, ritualists, and those in the social sciences. For example, as Catherine Bell says: "Ritualization always aligns one within a series of relationships linked to the ultimate sources of power."[21] The consideration of power relationships opens up another critical arena that is only beginning to be explored as a ritual question, but that has long been of primary concern to feminists.

Perhaps the older Ottonian approach is challenged by more than just the incursions of materialism, secularity, and moral deterioration. It would appear that it is not only under siege from without, but is eroding from within as women find their own ritual voice. To survive, the semitic traditions will almost surely have to make some accommodation with both the women in their midst—the lifeblood of Western religion, after all—and the culture that cradles and supports them.

Notes

1. Lawrence A. Hoffman, *Beyond the Text: A Holistic Approach to Liturgy* (Bloomington: Indiana University Press, 1987) 149-171.

2. Rudolf Otto, *The Idea of the Holy* (London: Oxford University Press, 1923).

3. See Mircea Eliade, *The Sacred and the Profane* (New York: Harcourt, Brace and Company, Inc., 1959).

4. Catherine Bell, "The Ritual Body and the Dynamics of Ritual Power," *Journal of Ritual Studies* 4:2: 299.

5. See Barbara Borts, "On Trespassing the Boundaries," chapter 4 in this volume.

6. See Carole Rayburn, "Ritual as Acceptance/Empowerment and Rejection/Disenfranchisement," chapter 7 in this volume.

7. Rosemary Radford Ruether, *Women-Church: Theory and Practice* (San Francisco, Harper & Row, 1985). The term originated with Elizabeth Schussler-Fiorenza. Earlier anthologies of feminist liturgies include Arlene Swidler, ed., *Sistercelebrations* (Philadelphia: Fortress Press, 1974); Sharon and Thomas Emswiler-Neufer's *Women and Wor-*

ship (New York: Harper & Row, 1974); and Ruth Duck, ed., *Bread for the Journey* (New York: Pilgrim Press, 1981, 1982).

8. Ruether, *Women-Church* 2.

9. The Women's Alliance for Theology, Ethics, and Ritual, in Washington, D.C.

10. Barbara G. Walker, *Women's Rituals: A Sourcebook* (HarperSan-Francisco, 1990). This approach, unfortunately, like that of Ruether and most feminist theologians, assumes that theory precedes practice, and that rituals can and should be created from whole cloth to serve the interests of theology. This is a dangerous and trivializing preassumption. Still, insofar as feminist theology proceeds directly from human experience, its suggested rituals may take root and flourish on a distinctly local basis. This, of course, would be completely consonant with the way in which women form and maintain religious communities.

11. Walker, *Women's Rituals* 91.

12. A parallel distinction has been made by Julia Kristeva, who observed the distinction between men's time and women's time: the former is linear, historical, teleological, progressive; the latter is cyclical, regenerative, eternal; see her "Women's Time" in *The Kriteva Reader*, trans. Toril Mor, ed. A. Jardin and H. Blake (New York: Columbia University Press, 1986, 187-213)). Jill Dubisch uses these categories to examine gender distinctions in the observation of a Greek pilgrimage ritual in her "Men's Time and Women's Time: History, Myth, and Ritual at a Modern Greek Shrine," *Journal of Ritual Studies* 5:1 (Winter 1991): 1-26.

13. Ruether, *Women-Church* 3.

14. As Proctor-Smith writes: "In gatherings of women, then, denominational, confessional, or traditional divisions are relativized" (*In Her Own Rite: Constructing Feminist Liturgical Tradition* [Nashville: Abingdon Press, 1990] 25). I would contend this relativizing process goes further, into the secular realm as well.

15. Church of St. Mary the Virgin, "Eucharistic Truth," in *The Anglican Digest* (Lent 1993): 21.

16. Diann Neu, "Women Revisioning Religious Rituals," chapter 11 in this volume.

17. Karen Sue Hybertsen, "Twisting Space: Women, Spirits, and Halloween," chapter 3 in this volume.

18. Lesley A. Northup, "Ritual Naming, Ritual Power: Forms of Address for Episcopal Women Clergy," paper presented to the Centennial Convention of the American Psychological Association, Washington, D.C., August 1992.

19. Ruether's work pointed to this theoretically: "Women-church embraces a liminal religiosity" (*Women-Church* 4).

20. See Carol A. Myscofski, "Women's Initiation Rites in Afro-Brazilian Religions: A Structural Source Analysis," *Journal of Ritual Studies* 2:1 (Winter 1988): 101-118.

21. Catherine Bell, *Ritual Theory, Ritual Practice* (New York: Oxford University Press, 1992) 141.

WOMEN'S RITUAL EVOLUTION

11

Women Revisioning Religious Rituals

Diann L. Neu

And she calls to us:
Come, share in my rituals.
Eat of my bread,
drink from my source,
take shelter in my wisdom,
be transformed by my fire,
and dance with the rhythm of the universe.
Blessed are you among women.

MANY WOMEN ARE REMEMBERING, REFORMING AND REVISIONING RE-
ligious rituals that are both personal and communal. Some are
creating and participating in new communities of feminist ritual, such as women-church; others are writing feminist
prayers, blessings, psalms, invocations, litanies, and creeds for
traditional worship services; still others are reclaiming matri-
archal spiritual sources, such as goddesses and their worship.

The Women's Movements have empowered women of diverse backgrounds to challenge most aspects of church and societal living concerning everything from biblical interpretation
to reproductive choice. Feminism has uncovered the inherently patriarchal nature of all structures of church and society
and has exposed the sexism which has been woven into the

very fabric of Christian and Jewish spiritualities, including religious rituals. A feminist religious revolution in ritual aims to reach forward to a new space and a new time that can heal dualisms of gender, mind/body/spirit, race/class/diversity, sexual preference/lifestyle, and secular/sacred.

Most women who revision religious ritual are involved in creating peaceful change for the global community, focusing on racism, class divisions and international solidarity as well as gender-related issues. We are activists and leaders in the ecology movement and environmental protection; we prioritize anti-racism and anti-apartheid efforts; we struggle to provide reproductive choice and disability rights; we insist on lesbian, gay and bisexual rights; we are active in healing, and ending the threat of nuclear contamination and destruction. It is from these concrete contemporary needs that we develop rituals.

Telling the Story: A Parable

A woman revisioning ritual is like a woman who decides to make a quilt. She first gathers fabric in her house—old blouses and dresses, curtains that don't fit the windows anymore, baby dresses and worn jeans, her partner's shirts, clothes that friends have left and never reclaimed, old dish towels and sheets. She designs a pattern. Then she reaches for her scissors. She cuts big pieces and little ones, long strips and short patches, perfectly square shapes and oddly cut ones. New shapes and sizes are offered to her by the old fabrics she has. Parts of her life, of her lover's life, of her children's lives, parts of her house and parts of her friends fall from her shears. Then she begins to arrange the patches into the pattern she has chosen and pin the fabric pieces to a backing cloth.

She discovers that she does not have enough pieces. The quilt will be too small, she thinks sadly. It just won't be big enough for her. She has another idea. She goes to buy new fabric so that she can cut bright strips and squares from it to continue her beautiful design. The woman hurries home, and gets out her scissors once again. She cuts more big pieces and little ones, long strips and short patches, perfectly square shapes and oddly cut ones. She takes the new pile of fragments, and begins to fit them in among the old pieces. Some look well together, others are harder to arrange. Finally the design looks just right.

But now she has a new worry. The quilt will be enormous. She realizes that she herself cannot do all the sewing to finish it. It would take more time than she has in her days, more time than is available in her weeks, her months, her life.

So she calls her friends. "Come and help me make a quilt," she says. They come. Some know just what to do. Others have never made a quilt before. Some call other friends, people who are strangers to her. They all bring needles. Those who are more experienced help the neophytes. Together they invent new ways to join the fabric. Some of them go out and bring back pieces of their lives. The quilt grows bigger and bigger. Babies sleep and play as their caresharers sew on the quilt. Children run and sing and learn their first stitches. Elders give advice and take their turns quilting.

Everyone sews and sews. The quilt grows larger and larger, brighter and bolder, more colorful and more diverse at every stitch. And the woman looks at the quilt which they are all making with their lives and she smiles and smiles, and she rejoices in her heart and is very glad.

Let those who have ears to hear, hear. Let those who have eyes to see, see. Let those who have hearts to feel, feel.

Revisioning Religious Ritual

This story captures my sense of what is happening to religious ritual as feminists reshape it. Women are gathering individually and collectively to revision a deep spiritual awareness that integrates the old and the new. Ritual revision implies the necessity of ritual criticism and the possibility of ritual ineptness. I suggest the following five basic approaches as an outline of the many ways women are bringing feminist insights to ritual. There may, of course, be others, some perhaps that you use and do not see here, but the general schema is as follows.

First, women are bringing feminist concerns to institutional religious services. We work for inclusivity that reflects women as imaging the divine in all aspects of worship: inclusive language, inclusive cast, and inclusive celebrations. Second, women are reclaiming and redesigning traditional ritual systems and symbols. We create and celebrate anew feminist eucharists, seders, baptisms, commitment ceremonies, funeral services, and more to allow more meaningful and clear incorporation of women's experience of the sacred. Third, women are creating new ceremonies that express women's spiritual experiences. We celebrate transitions in women's life cycles: menarche, reproductive choices, miscarriage, stillbirth, birthing, adoption, divorce, career change, loss of friendship, leaving a religious congregation, handfasting (commitment), menopause, croning, entering a nursing home, and death. Fourth, women are integrating politics and justice with ritual. We incorporate symbol and ritual into public demonstrations, marches and protests that decry injustice and demand change. Fifth, women are attending to healing. We are designing communal healings that support women surviving rape, incest, domestic violence, hysterectomies, AIDS, mastectomies, addictions, illness, and choices made that they are grieving.

Naming Principles of Feminist Ritual-Making

Patch #1: Feminist rituals value both the process and the product.

Quilt-makers reveal that there is an amazing amount of energy available to people who get pleasure from what they are doing and find meaning in the work itself. The process of creating ever deepening and inclusive ritual is usually as transformative as celebrating the ritual itself, and sometimes more so. It requires faithfulness to the collective mode: listening into the stories of one another's truths and leaning into the winds of one another's diversities. Women design rituals with others to give rise to this diversity and creativity. Working together, women cross over into another land: the richness of other cultures; we cross over into another time: the ancient past and feminist future of female lineage; we cross over into another path: standing together against injustice and celebrating together women's ways. Process and product are interconnected. Together they inspire passion.

Patch #2: Feminist rituals focus on relationships that liberate and empower women, as well as supportive men and children who are moving from patriarchy to full humanity.

Quilts convey the intimate relationships between the quilters and the quilt. Quilting is a communal art. Like it, feminist religious rituals are inherently connective, providing integration of several kinds: the self with itself as it contemplates its movements through biological and historical change; the self with the culture, by the use of familiar, often axiomatic common symbols; and the self with others, joining celebrants into an often profound community where all manner of distinctions may be transcended in an all-embracing sacred unity.

As women approach ritual-making, we bring with us a healthy hermeneutics of suspicion concerning each culture's relationship with women. We remain suspicious of all cultural materials, including scripture, because time and again women's stories and experiences, along with those of other oppressed peoples, have been systematically written out of history. Thus, feminist ritual-makers search for, recover, and create aspects of women's cultural experiences that have been forgotten, censored, or negated in the creation and transmission of culture. We affirm the integrity of women's relationships and their expressions as revealed in art, song, dance, story, and image. We must read and sing, create and recreate texts by women to remember our stories and recover feminist collective memory.

Women's relationships with one another are valued and affirmed in feminist rituals as imaging the divine. The memory and meaning of women's experiences are shared and passed on by naming women in litanies, telling women's stories, singing women's songs, and praying with female images of the holy. Feminist rituals encourage and reinforce a global sisterhood which interacts with all generations of women: those before, those living now, and those yet to come. They strengthen women's solidarity with one another and embolden women to identify with all women and to act on behalf of women everywhere.

Patch #3: Feminist religious rituals share power among all participants.

In quilts, the startling balance of one kind of energy coexisting with a very different one captures our imagination. The quilt, with all of its pieces sewn together, communicates its power. In creating a communal quilt or a feminist ritual, patterns of leadership and responsibility reflect mutuality among all participants, both in the collaborative process of planning and in the community event of creating and celebrating. Each woman chooses to use her authority as she wishes for the preparation and enactment of the event.

Feminist ritual is effected through the communal interaction of participants sharing leadership skills that reside in each member, not in one presider. Some design the content of the celebration; visual artists create the ritual environment; writers compose the blessings; musicians play or write the songs; others gather the symbols; some tell the stories, proclaim the readings, voice the poems or mime the message; and dancers interpret the music and move to the rhythm of the ceremony. During the ritual, different people have responsibility for initiating each part when they think it is appropriate to do so. Participants are invited to share their power throughout a ritual in spontaneous and self-generated responses: by sharing symbols, by responding to a question, by adding to a litany, by creating a blessing.

Verbal and non-verbal interactions are mutually empowering. Readings include concepts and language which are egalitarian. Gestures reflect equality, not dominance or submission. The ritual includes a time for "Reflecting Together" when a question is asked that flows from the theme. For example, during a Harvest celebration, "Deep Peace of Changing Seasons To You,"[1] WATER's Women-Church ritual group reflected together on "How do you describe your connection to your religious past, to your spiritual future? Think for a moment, then turn to someone next to you and share whatever part of your reflection you wish." Reflective questions invite participants to share their spiritual power. They replace homilies and sermons which model one person only as having the power to reflect on the theme of the ritual.

Ritual spaces are chosen and designed to reflect shared power, too. Feminist rituals are celebrated in a circle to convey that shared power resides in the participants who are each equi-distant from the center of the circle. When tables are used for altars, circular ones are preferred. When candles for participants are placed on the altar, they are arranged in a circle around or beside other symbols. Circles and spirals, spheres and squares embrace multiple energies and powers.

Patch #4: Feminist religious rituals use symbols and stories, images and words, gestures and dances, along with a variety of art forms which emerge from women's ways of knowing.

Quilt-makers are artists who design and redesign patterns from both old and new fabric. Feminist ritual-makers use age-old symbols and new age ones with a feminist insight. Candles symbolize the preservation of the soul and the spark of revolution. Maypoles reclaim women's fertility. Breaking sticks signifies letting go of women's suffering. Putting evergreen branches around a room creates a safe place. Quilts represent women's lives. Every symbol has potential for use in ritual.

Feminist eucharists use a variety of breads and drinks to express the diversity of communities: unleavened bread to recall refugees and exiles, grape juice to signify solidarity with those freeing themselves from dependence on alcohol, tortillas to symbolize Central American people, red wine to recall the blood of martyrs, cornbread to represent indigenous peoples, apple juice to reclaim all women as holy, beginning with Eve.

The texts used in feminist rituals are works composed by women. Stories, poems, readings, exorcisms, invocations, blessings, songs, psalms, and prayers are either written by women for the occasion or found in the growing body of women's work that is plentiful, available, and powerful.

Patch #5: Feminist religious rituals value women's bodies as vehicles of divine revelation, and honor women in all our diversity as imaging the divine and as engaging in divine activity.

Quilts are personal documents that honor relationships. They can be seen, touched, and smelled. Feminist religious rituals express embodied knowledge through kinesthetic, auditory, and visual pathways which make it safer for persons with disabilities to participate, and they provide an arena for everyone to experience the divine in her own embodied way. Sight, sound, touch, smell, body movements and tactile objects are employed to engage participants in ritual meaning. People pour water, ring bells, offer an embrace, burn incense, move in procession, eat bread and drink wine to emphasize embodied action during ritual.

Names for the divine used for blessings and invocations in feminist rituals move beyond Mother or Father, She or He, to include attributes for the divine that are appropriate for the given ritual. Examples include Passionate Spirit, Holy One of Peace, Source of Wisdom, Liberator of the Oppressed, Companion on the Journey, Goddess of Laughter, and Beautiful Spirit. Using attributes such as these expands

our concept of the divine, enables women to picture ourselves as passionate, holy, wise, and beautiful, and honors
women as imaging the divine.

Women's sexual and sensual experiences form the content
of many feminist rituals. "You Are Not Alone"[2] offers three
ritual experiences that affirm women's reproductive choices:
seeking wisdom when a woman experiences an unintended
pregnancy, affirming a woman's choice for abortion, and
awaiting the birth of a woman's baby. In the ritual of awaiting
birth, milk, bread and fruit are blessed. One woman, pouring
milk into the glass, prays:

> Mother's milk of union,
> Earliest sacred communion.
> Let us together touch and bless this life-force.
>> Blessed are you, Source of Life, for you desire health, safety
>> and well-being for your offspring.

>> Another woman takes the bread and prays:
> Bread of life,
> Nurturing, sustaining, Grandma's life.
> Touch and bless this common thread.
>> Blessed are you, Bakerwoman Goddess, for you give your
>> loved ones food for the journey.

>> Another woman takes the fruit and prays:
> Fruit of blessing,
> Patience, strength, love abounding.
> Touch and bless this desirous food.
>> Blessed are you, Sweet Friend, for you empower birthing sis-
>> ters with blessings.
> Let us eat, drink and celebrate together.

*Patch #6: Feminist religious rituals motivate and legitimate social
transformation.*

Quilting is transformative activity. Quilters imagine new designs and yet must choose one. Working on a quilt tells you
something about the life you have lived and the things you
have come to value. Feminist religious rituals urge participants to transform the unnatural divisions of class, race, sexual orientation and culture. Exorcisms are used to strengthen
participants in their work to overcome the evils of racism,
classism, sexism, heterosexism, ableism and ageism that bind

women everywhere. The "Exorcism" from "Women of Fire: a Pentecost Event"[3] begins:

> The pains, hurts and alienations of one woman belong to all women. From all of these we exorcise our race—the race of women—on this day of Pentecost.
> We respond to each evil by saying three times in our own language the words: "Be gone! Be gone! Be gone!"
> 1. The consistently male image of God—
>   "Be gone! Be gone! Be gone!"
> 2. Structures of racism and apartheid that separate black and white women, European and Mediterranean women—
>   "Be gone! Be gone! Be gone!"
> 3. Seeing women's bodies and souls as dirty, sinful and inferior—
>   "Be gone! Be gone! Be gone!"
> 4. Jealousy and aggression that separate woman from woman, sister from sister—
>   "Be gone! Be gone! Be gone!"
> 5. All forms of patriarchy that suffocate women's spirits—
>   "Be gone! Be gone! Be gone!"
> 6. Unequal pay scales for women—
>   "Be gone! Be gone! Be gone!"
> 7. Chains of classism, heterosexism and ageism that bind women everywhere—
>   "Be gone! Be gone! Be gone!"
> 8. The stereotyping of women that does violence—
>   "Be gone! Be gone! Be gone!"
> 9. Trafficking in women and forced prostitution that uses women as sexual objects—
>   "Be gone! Be gone! Be gone!"
> 10. The fears women have of our own natural powers—
>   "Be gone! Be gone! Be gone!"

Language used in feminist ritual encourages social change. Texts and participants speak of women and men, and name women first to signify a change in the power dynamic. They name Sarah, Hagar and Abraham as well as the other matriarchs and patriarchs. They replace racist words such as light and dark with fire and shadow, sunrise and sunset. Aware of able-bodied words, they use all instead of whole, insensitivity instead of blindness, dreams instead of visions, indifference instead of deafness. Real inclusivity includes communicating in a variety of languages.

The ritual, "Re-igniting Fires of Justice,"[4] challenges participants to unlearn layers of racism, to interrupt this oppression,
to rise from the ashes of destruction, and to re-ignite fires of
justice. The "Sending Forth" from this ritual urges social
transformation:

Let us rise again from ashes,
　　from anger that we have felt,
　　from dreams we have not fully dreamed.
　　　　Let us re-ignite fires of justice.
　　　　Response: Let us re-ignite fires of justice.

Let us rise again from ashes,
　　from the good that we have not done,
　　from the pain and suffering we have known.
　　　　Let us re-ignite fires of justice.
　　　　Response: Let us re-ignite fires of justice.

Let us rise again from ashes,
　　from the narrow boundaries of our lives
　　from the lies that have kept us divided.
　　　　Let us re-ignite fires of justice.
　　　　Response: Let us re-ignite fires of justice.

Let us rise again from ashes . . . How else shall we rise and re-
ignite fires of justice? Tell us.

Let us rise again from ashes . . . (Sharing.)

Re-igniting fires of justice, let us go forth from this place to
fast from racism, to weep for injustice, to mourn with ashes, to
re-ignite fires of justice. Amen. Blessed Be. Let It Be So.

*Patch #7: In feminist religious rituals, politics, justice and incultu-
ration interrelate as friendly companions for feminist change.*

Quilters show the powerful urge to make patterns out of the
ordinary that speak something very profound. The love of the
ordinary blazes out the backyard miracle: Ohio Sunflower,
Texas Star, Snail's Track, Sweet Green Leaf. Feminist rituals
celebrate the ordinary, and call participants to something new.
They attempt to express the varieties of human experience that
exist globally: diversity in culture, class, race, sexual preference, lifestyle. They provide a place where participants contact
true justice to self, others, and the global community.

We incorporate symbol and ritual into public demonstrations, marches and protests. During World AIDS Day, 1 De-

cember, and when the Names Quilt is unrolled, we celebrate the ritual "Telling Love's Story: Remembering and Responding to AIDS"[5] and we pray:

> Compassionate Holy One, open our hearts and minds and hands so that we may connect ourselves to the global community of others responding to AIDS as we pray:
>
> We remember all those women, men and children in this country and around the world who are living with AIDS.
> Please respond: Justice demands that we remember and respond.
>
> We remember all who care for people living and dying with AIDS in their homes, in hospices and in support centers. Response: Justice demands that we remember and respond.
>
> We remember all who are involved in research and hospital care that they may respect the dignity of each person. Response: Justice demands that we remember and respond.
>
> We remember all partners who are left mourning for their beloved ones. Response: Justice demands that we remember and respond.
>
> We remember all parents who learn the truth of their children's lives through their process of facing death. Response: Justice demands that we remember and respond.
>
> We remember . . . Please finish the sentence and we will respond.

Patch #8: Feminist religious rituals value women's solidarity with one another and strengthen these bonds in community for overcoming violence in all its forms.

Quilts are guides that help us work our way out of a labyrinth. Feminist rituals alter our ordinary sense of time and, like art, let us lose ourselves and step out of our usual conscious, critical mentality. They challenge women to active engagement on women's behalf in the social and political arena.

Healing rituals support women surviving violence in all of its forms: rape, incest, domestic violence, ritual abuse. They include exorcisms, shouting, moaning, yelling, stomping, kicking, and outcries of injustice and lament.

Feminist rituals name evil and reject violence in all of its forms. Women are creating rituals of support and healing for survivors of abuse. "Creating A Safe Place" sets the tone for the ritual, "Like Drops of Water."[6]

Let us create a safe place where we can celebrate a ritual of healing that we need. Why do you need safe places? (Pause.) Please respond to each phrase with "We need safe places."

Because violence exists in the world, we need safe places.

Because women and children have been violated . . .

Because in the U.S. a woman is battered every 15 seconds . . .

Because a rape is committed every six minutes . . .

Because one woman in four will be sexually assaulted in her lifetime . . .

Because half the victims of sexual abuse are under age eleven . . .

Because one out of every seven married women is the victim of marital rape . . .

Because twenty-five percent of college women experience rape or attempted rape . . .

Why else do we need safe places? Tell us and we will respond with "we need safe places."

The "Sending Forth" that closes this ritual emphasizes the message of the poems, stories, and songs:

Let us go forth from this safe place filled with support for one another. When times are tough—and they will be—let us remember that this time we are not alone.

Let us go forth from this safe place committed to working to create a world where abuse is non-existent.

Let us go forth from this safe place remembering we are like drops of water . . . and the water comes again.

Patch #9: Feminist religious rituals share with children a feminist faith that models a life-stance of love and justice.

Quilts are made for children and children help make quilts. Children participate in feminist rituals and some rituals are designed especially for children. Young children have grown up in our local women-church group. Nursing infants come at their mother's breast. During our gatherings they often meet separately for a different, yet similar, storytelling time and then they are involved in an activity that follows the theme of the ritual: drawing pictures, making crowns, learning a song, or creating a dance. In this way women pass on a feminist faith to the next generations and children receive an integrated, just and wholistic perspective of life.

A favorite memory occurred during WATER's Seder, "Miriam's Sisters Rejoice."[7] Chris Schüssler Fiorenza, then nine years old, asked these questions and Mary E. Hunt responded:

1. Mother, why is this night different from all other nights? Why do we celebrate a Seder telling the stories of women?
Response: This night is different because people gather to hold life in its contradictions—

    the bitter and the sweet,
    the death and resurrection,
    the struggle and the victory,
    the reality of war and the desperate efforts for peace.

We do this as women with our friends for, as Miriam's sisters, we believe that only by empowering women can we make every night like this night—a time for celebration and enjoyment, for reflection and letting go. We set this night aside as a foretaste of our unity to come.

2. Mother, why do we taste this bitterness and keep it fresh in our mouths?
Response: Life is bitter at times, there is evil in the world. Look to Central America and the Middle East. Think of those who are sick, and those who have died this year. Think of rape and incest, of our own failings (add more as the year's events warrant.) These are bitter realities!!

But there is hope, too, and we keep our eyes and our ears and our hearts open to the fresh new life that this season signals. We hold these contradictions together because that is life.

3. Mother, why do we then taste both salt tears and sweet?
Response: Salt tears and sweet together remind us that just as a friend comforts you when you cry, so, too, does the world provide you with help. No burden is too heavy for all of us to carry, no command to do justice is too difficult if we as women bond together to do justice. That is why we take the bitter with the sweet, together, knowing that we can carry on.

4. Mother, why do we find it so difficult to lean back and relax during this meal?
Response: It is fun to sing and eat and party together, but deep in the back of our minds is the news of war on TV, the reality of women's suffering, the destruction of the earth that we love. We try to relax, and we do. But we are always vigilant, on edge, so as to be ready to spring into action for justice.

Praying in Rituals

Many of the principles cited above suggest a variety of prayer forms. In feminist religious rituals, women are creating and re-creating prayer forms that we can begin to name and recognize.

Naming the Circle: As a ritual begins, it is important that participants introduce themselves to those with whom they are gathering. This facilitates community bonding that enables ritual celebration. Naming sets the tone for the ritual. For "Come to Waters of Peace,"[8] the "Naming Ceremony" begins:

> Women, men and children around the world work that peace with justice may prevail. Let us say our names and, in solidarity with peacemakers, speak the name of peacemakers. I am Diann. I bring into our circle the Co-Madres of El Salvador and the Mothers of the Plaza de Mayo of Argentina, the mothers of the disappeared and political prisoners.

Litany: Litanies are ancient prayer forms, sung or said, that invite an affixed response from those gathered. These two litanies are central to the ritual, "Signs of Trouble and Beauty."[9]

Litany of Trouble

Our response is: "And then there is women-church."
In my life there is spiritual hunger . . .
In my life there is loneliness . . .
In my life there is patriarchy . . .
In my life there is fury . . .
In my life there are closed doors . . .
In my life there are patronizing situations . . .
In my life there are oppressive structures . . .
In my life there are few who really listen. . .
In my life there are poverty, unequal pay and little or no pay. . .
In my life there are unused talents . . .
In my life there is a search for community . . .
In my life there are hidden treasures . . .
   Please add others . . .

Litany of Beauty

After each line please respond by saying: "Women-church is powerful." Soothed by the oil and connected to this community we affirm:
In my life there is community . . .
In my life there is joy to share . . .
In my life there are endless possibilities . . .
In my life there are moments of strength . . .
In my life there is a spiritual home . . .
In my life there is shared love . . .
In my life there are liberating struggles . . .

In my life there are people who "hear me into speech . . ."
In my life there is a wealth through resource sharing and
    networking . . .
In my life there is freedom to use and develop my skills . . .
In my life there is a circle of friendship . . .
    Please add others . . .

Invoking the Holy: Invocations beseech the divine to acknowledge holy presence or to ask for help. They are often used to gather the participants and focus the message of the ritual in prayer. This "Gathering Prayer" is prayed in "Harvesting Peace."[10]

(Seven different people pray each sentence.)

O Holy One of Peace, we gather with your people around the earth to harvest peace.

We gather with your people of the Middle East where Arab, Jewish and Christian people find peace an unattainable goal.

We gather with your people of Germany where unification is a small sign of hope.

We gather with your people of Central America where the beauty of the land is mixed with the blood of the martyrs.

We gather with your people of South Africa where violence and bloodshed continue.

We gather as your people of the United States feeling a deep responsibility to bring about peace starting in our own neighborhoods, especially in the nation's capital where murders continue unabated.

We gather with your people through the ages who have turned swords into plowshares that peace may be harvested.

Lighting a Candle: Feminist rituals often begin or include a lighting of candles, a custom that is intimately associated with religious ceremonies. Candle light puts participants in touch with the spirit world and wards off demons and negativity. This "Lighting Candles" closes the ritual "Telling Love's Story: Remembering and Responding to AIDS."[11]

(One person takes a small candle, lights it from the large one, places it starting a circle around the large one and says:) I light a candle of _____, e.g., hope. Come, take a candle, light it saying, "I light a candle of _____, e.g., forgiveness, thanks, sorrow. (Candle lighting and sharing.)
(When all candles are lighted, she continues:)
We bring together many candles, many lights.

As those who keep the night watch await the dawn, we remain vigilant,
> Until a cure for AIDS is found,
> Until those dying with AIDS are comforted,
> Until truth sets us free,
> Until love drives out injustice,

We shall not give up the fight.

Blessing of Bread: Any symbol can be blessed in ritual. Bread, a eucharistic symbol of tablesharing, is a common one. This blessing of bread is offered in "Women Crossing Worlds: In Solidarity and Friendship."[12]

> Remember this feeling as we take, bless, break and eat bread together. (Four people speak a sentence similar to the following as they each bring bread to the table: tortillas, wheat bread, rye bread, matzah.)
> Voice 1: Daily bread in every land is the bread of necessity, the bread of life.
> Voice 2: Women bake bread daily: tortillas, wheat bread, rye bread, matzah.
> Voice 3: Women are as common as these common, daily breads.
> Voice 4: When you see bread, bake bread, eat bread, remember the women of the world.
> Let us extend our hands, palms up, and bless these breads. (Silent blessing.) Let us pass these breads around, take pieces of them, and eat as we listen.

Recalling Women's Words: Readings, stories, litanies and prayers often recall women's words to keep their memory and wisdom ever present. In "The Saving Grace of Fun"[13] the "Blessing for the Wine and Juice" recalls the words of Julian of Norwich:

> This fruit of the vine symbolizes strength and happiness. Let us extend our hands and bless it listening to the words of our sister Julian.
>
> > It is God's will
> > that we do all in our power
> > to keep ourselves strong
> > for happiness is everlasting
> > and pain is passing and will end.
> > Therefore it is not God's will
> > that we pine and mourn
> > over feelings of pain

> but that we get better
> and continue to enjoy life.

Blessing Ritual Participants: Feminist rituals include a blessing of one another that includes a full body hug, a blessing of hands, an honoring of one another, eye contact around the circle, smudging with herbs or incense, passing a candle, or sharing a symbol. This Blessing from "Affirming A Choice"[14] extends the power of the ritual.

> _____ (name of woman), we love you very deeply. As a sign of our affirmation of you and of your choice, we give you this bowl and this oil. Oil soothes bones that are weary from making a difficult decision. Oil strengthens and heals. Oil . . . (add sentences that reflect what the woman spoke in her story.)
>
> We bless you with this oil. Come, friends, take oil from the bowl and massage _____'s (the woman's name) hands, face, feet, neck, shoulders and head. Close your blessing by embracing her.
>
> _____ (name of woman), the bowl is a tangible symbol of this day. When times are difficult—and such days come to each of us—look at this bowl and remember our love for you. We bless you, _____ (name of the woman), and promise to be with you on your way.

Final Blessing: The final blessing gathers the message of the ritual and sends participants forth with a charge to participate in social transformation. This final "Litany of Leavetaking" closes as follows in "In Praise of Women's Harvest":[15]

> The time of saying goodbye is here. This day we have shared our stories, and celebrated our harvests. As we close, let us leave one another with a word or phrase that is our blessing for this time together. Let us speak our name and our word. (Sharing.)

Sending Forth: Women revisioning religious rituals are rekindling fires of renewal that are centuries overdue. We give hope to spiritually hungry women, and provide shelter for the spiritually homeless. Feminist religious rituals express feminist values of inclusivity and justice. They invite participation in a feminist dream of a new dawn where we host a worldwide party and feed the hungry of every nation. They challenge us to call our friends together to create a ninepatch quilt that will swaddle our babies, teach skills to our children, warm our old people and provide community for us all.

And she sends us forth:
Go, share my rituals.
Eat of my bread,
drink from my source,
take shelter in my wisdom,
be transformed by my fire,
and dance with the rhythm of the universe.
Blessed are you among women.

Notes

1. Diann Neu, "Deep Peace of Changing Seasons to You," *WATERwheel* 5:2 (Summer-Fall 1992): 4-5.

2. Diann Neu, "You Are Not Alone," *WATERwheel* 4:4 (Winter 1991-1992): 4-5.

3. Diann Neu, "Women of Fire: A Pentecost Event" (WATERworks Press, 1990) 30.

4. Diann Neu, "Re-igniting Fires of Justice," *WATERwheel* 5:1 (Spring 1992): 4-5.

5. Diann Neu, "Telling Love's Story: Remembering and Responding to AIDS," *WATERwheel* 5:3 (Fall 1992): 4-5.

6. Diann Neu, "Like Drops of Water," *WATERwheel* 4:1 (Spring 1991): 4-5. Statistics from *The Flyer* (Winter 1990-1991).

7. Diann Neu, Mindy Shapiro, Barbara Cullom, Tobie Hoffman, "Miriam's Sisters Rejoice" (WATERworks Press, 1988). Responses to all questions by Mary E. Hunt, spoken to Chris Schussler Fiorenza at WATER's first Seder in 1985.

8. Diann Neu, "Come to Waters of Peace," *WATERwheel* 3:4 (Winter 1990-1991): 4-5.

9. Diann Neu, "Signs of Trouble and Beauty," *Women and the Gospel Traditions* (WATERworks Press, 1989) 9-10.

10. Diann Neu, "Harvesting Peace" *WATERwheel* 3:3 (Fall 1990): 4-5.

11. Diann Neu, "Telling Love's Story: Remembering and Responding to AIDS," *WATERwheel* 5:3 (Fall 1992): 4-5.

12. Diann Neu, "Women Crossing Worlds: In Solidarity and Friendship," *WATERwheel* 2:4 (Winter 1989-1990) 4-5.

13. Diann Neu and Mary E. Hunt, "The Saving Grace of Fun," *WATERwheel* 1:2 (Summer 1988) 4-5.

14. Diann Neu, "You Are Not Alone," *WATERwheel* 4:4 (Winter 1991-1992) 4-5.

15. Diann Neu, "In Praise of Women's Harvest," *WATERwheel* 4:2 (Summer-Fall 1991) 4-5.

12
Womanist Ritual

Amitiyah Elayne Hyman

Thus she had lain
Sugarcane sweet
Deserts her hair
Golden her feet
Mountains her breasts
Two Niles her tears
Thus she has lain
Black through the years.

Over the white seas
Rime white and cold
Brigands ungentled
Icicle bold
Took her young daughters
Stole her strong sons
Churched her with Jesus
Then bled her with guns
Thus she has lain.

Now she is rising
Remember her pain
Remember her losses
Her screams loud and vain
Remember her riches
Her history slain
Now she is striding
Although she had lain.[1]

WE AFRICAN-AMERICAN FEMALES CARRY WITHIN OUR GENES THE RA-
cial memory of an Afrocentric understanding of the periods
and passages of our lives. At Melanin Scholars Conferences in
New York City and Washington, D.C., in 1988 and 1989 respec-
tively, psychologists, educators, anthropologists, and others
made data available which confirms that high levels of a body
chemical called melanin, found in large doses in African people, enhance the human capacity to use all the senses and to
do physical things very well. Moreover "accessing one's un-
conscious is easier for persons who have high levels of melanin."[2] Assisted by melanin, when we have the will and recognize the necessity, we can remember episodes and events from
our collective past which reinforce our cultural understanding. We have the capacity to be the bearers of culture for our
communities. For many, this knowing is a faint and faded
memory. We have suffered the debilitating malady of racio-
cultural amnesia which has rendered us pale shadows of our
former selves and left us easy prey for the manipulation and
indoctrination of the larger socio-cultural context in which we
find ourselves. We have become imitators of others and largely useless to our own people. Others of us, by virtue of "disad-
vantage," intentional struggle, or generous mentoring, have
escaped the programing and apprehend more fully who we
are as herstorical people. Fortunately, whether we have forgotten or remembered together, we can assist one another in the
long-overdue healing that the acts of remembering afford.

Ritual is a bridge by which those of us who have almost forgotten and those of us who know can cross over into remembering who we were, whose we are, and who we are intended
to become. Ritual can assist us by naming and validating the
essential worth of our experience. In our collective search for
meaning, relatedness, worth, and assurance, we are anchored
by ritual.

> Ritual is not a bad thing. It allows people to make a metaphoric
> statement about the paradoxes and the contradictions of the hu-
> man situation. Ritual provides an opportunity to connect with
> others who share the same experience, allowing a recollection
> of experiences.[3]

We understand and do not need to argue the necessity for
reinforcing our own human experience. For African-American

females, there are rites of passage that can serve to sustain us as a battle-scarred and demeaned people, travelling in a strange land. Several hundred of years of slavery and patriarchal subjugation have taken their toll. During the height of the black-led Civil Rights struggle of the 1960s, when we were energized to fight for our freedom, before the marching and the acts of non-violent confrontation began, we always grounded ourselves in heavily ritualized acts of worship. We gathered in churches to engage first in songs of protest and praise; we first sought out the God of our understanding to become energized for the struggle ahead.

However, the habits of dependency and despondency relearned in the 1970s and 1980s have contributed much to erasing the life- affirming and esteem-building habits of our richly ritualized people. The rituals developed to give meaning and posit value to the people of America were not created with Africans in mind. Much of what has sustained us and "brought us over" has been coopted and commercialized, culture for sale and profit, not for living.

In identifying womanist ritual for living that will work for contemporary African-American women and girls, who jump the double-dutch difficulties of race and sex, we look to using ceremonial signs and symbols in repetitive, yet improvisational, ways. We choose those rituals that come out of the past and our common life together in another place and time. The reference of a past life, begun in the Motherland of Africa and continued in the diaspora, helps us to reinforce values and ways of being that allow us to transcend the present crisis of our people.

To Go Back to Tradition Is the First Step Forward[4]

The necessity for adaptation of our rituals to the present diaspora reality assures us that they will be vibrant and lively for a people of today. Improvisation, flexibility, and cultural agility are the means by which we adapt. Such rituals, based on our former life but adapted to our present one, help us to create a feeling of togetherness, to suggest that our togetherness has some useful purpose; and therefore to give ourselves permission to experience some emotional and spiritual enrichment by our coming together.

The ways in which African-American women have traditionally come together are numerous and diverse. In ceremonies and celebrations that attend the passages of our lives, such as birth, puberty, marriage, child-bearing, eldership, and death, we have gathered to braid our hair, to prepare food for communal meals, to dress ourselves for special occasions like weddings, funerals, and homecomings. Nevertheless, these same habits of African women—to gather around one another to braid hair, to groom ourselves, to exchange gossip and communal wisdom in the safety called village—is at risk of being lost. At younger and younger ages, our girls are replacing it with the ritual of showing up for an appointment in hair salons; there, an African- American girl sits alone with her hairdresser and occupies herself with magazines while taking the "kinks" out beneath the dryer—whose very design necessitates isolation and solitary preoccupation. She gets her ideas from the written page, not the word spoken to address her directly. She never hears her own name called out nor does she get help in customizing the standards and norms of the magazine to the shape and circumference of her own life experience. Messages conveyed by author and photographer are created by those who have no necessary accountability to her nor any direct investment in her appropriation of them. Lost is any notion of the sacredness of her person, whose essential value is demonstrated by the coming together of friends and family to lay hands upon her head and help to fashion her beauty, while sharing secrets and advice for living. Gone is the good feeling of being in community and the soothing recognition that she "belongs" because she joins in.

Locating ourselves within the bosom of the Motherland, both geographically and ritualistically, helps to create a safety zone or sanctuary space where we can find refuge, retreat, refreshment, and revitalization to advance along the journey. Our rituals begin in circling ourselves together, each sister on parity with the other. We claim each other in straight-eyed embrace, hands able to reach out for one another at the impulse of spirits. Our circle is able to expand or contract, making easy adjustments to the size of our sisterhood at any given moment. We are both connected and open to the newest member. Having formed ourselves in circle we are ready to listen.

The sound of our own hearts beating is rhythmically set by

the drum, the heartbeat of the community. It sets the body to life and assures that blood and vitality will flow. The drumming may be that of hands clapping together, feet shuffling or stomping, or hands hitting a skin stretched over a hollowed-out log. This pulsating beat is the mud line, the baseline, the essential heart's beat. Even a palpitating heart can set the rhythm for our circle. When we listen closely, we hear a beat in the fluttering. Our bodies can begin to move in time with the beating of the drum, allowing us to feel the vibration and let it move through us.

As the vibrations rise through our bodies, they build to the necessity of breath, deep and full. The energies that cannot escape through hands and feet, swaying hips, heaving shoulders and nodding heads, find their utterance through vocal cords. We moan, we cry, we shout, we laugh, we sing. We glory in the joy of feeling the healing effects of allowing the vibrations of sound to run through our bodies.[5] Slowly we begin to sing ourselves into sense and meaning. Our singing is not bound by "lines and dots."[6] In some instances it may more closely resemble shouting.

> Broadly speaking, shouting is an emotional explosion, responsive to rhythm. It is called forth by sung rhythm, spoken rhythm, humming rhythm, the foot patting or hand-clapping. Shouting is a community thing. It thrives in concert. Rhythm is increasing with each shouter who communicated fervor to someone else. Women shout more frequently than men.[7]

We understand intuitively and encourage one another emphatically, instructed by the proverb:

> If you can walk, you can dance;
> If you can talk, you can sing.[8]

and

> If you can sing, you can shout.

> > DeeDee said she wouldn't shout in
> > church
> > unlessen
> > the Spirit hit her in such a way
> > she couldn't
> > help herself
> > (what other way she think it happen)

cause...
shouting
was not her uncool thing.
not necessary
smile, pat yo feet, clap yo hands
and say amen (not too loud) please
Spirit hit her
it did
knocked her down
sat her upright again
opened her mouth
made a shout come out
and left her sitting
wide-eyes at all the "saints"
who had prayed that one
day
DeeDee would know what they meant
when they sang
i can't holt it
i can't help it
"feel like fire in my bones"
if'fen i don't shout
i feel like i might
turn to stone,
even, the rocks
can
cry out.[9]

Learning to "shout" is learning to reproduce an authentically African phenomenon. It comes to us from the Motherland through the Black diaspora of slavery as an accommodation to our New World reality.

At night many slave families went to one another's houses to hold prayer meetings and to sing and "shout". The shout was a series of body motions (usually described as a dance by outsiders) that the slaves performed to the accompaniment of spirituals. It exemplified the creative Afro-Carolinian adaptation of a West African ring dance performed to complex drum rhythms. In the New World the drums, upon which Africans had relied to articulate their spiritual life, were lost; but a substitute was improvised with polyrythmic hand-clapping and foot-stamping. The slaves called the adaptation "shouting," after the African "saut", meaning to walk or run around. Similar expressive behavior was widespread among blacks in the Caribbean and elsewhere in the South Carolina low country.[10]

In this highly ritualized way we remind one another of who we are, how far we've travelled, how high it is, how wide. As the sound of our individual voices builds in us, we throw it forward into the circle, like the slaves did long ago, gathering down in the woods with their iron pots to hold it. Likewise we create a wall of sound whose sum is greater than our individual parts. We make song in this moment, the tune and tenor of which are great enough that each of us will have something to carry away, some way to carry on, even after we part from one another. We may remain in this formation for hours, sustained by our singing. Melody lines and lead parts are traded around the circle according to the rise and fall of spirits. Voices stack up around each other.[11] Whenever a sister risks stepping out with her sound, she can be assured that others will be with her, coming in with complementary sounds over and under hers. We create harmony in this way, blending into one another and moving as quickly away to form rhythms and polyrhythms appropriate to the meanings we seek to convey. At times like these there is no time. We lose our westernized minds to enter into the now of our Africanity.

Unless the People Sing, the Spirit Can't Descend[12]

Such singing is indeed African. It becomes our religion. In his work, *Slave Religion: The Invisible Institution of the Ante-Bellum South*, scholar Albert Raboteau reminds us that

> the most obvious continuity between African and Afro-American religions is the style of performance in ritual action. Drumming, singing, and dancing are essential features of African and Afro-American liturgical expression.[13]

It allows for a coming together of ourselves, separated into physical, emotional, mental and spiritual beings, into oneness as whole humans. Rooted in another time and place, it gives us permission to live in the here and now as unapologetically black and proud African-Americans. The a capella ensembles Sweet Honey in the Rock and In Process and other such community-based groups demonstrate this kind of ritual and revival in a performance space. Douglas S. Barasch shares the insights of one group's founder, Bernice Johnson Reagon, in a recent *New York Times* article:

Sweet Honey concerts draw on the same kind of spontaneity and spirituality. "We're actually creating something in the way that I understand ritual and ceremonies to be," she says. "You know the structure. You know what you have to do, but it doesn't exist before you do it . . . and once you do it, it's gone. You never repeat it."[14]

While we cannot repeat it, each time we gather in this way, it reminds us that our kinkiness is God-created, and to be celebrated. We remember that it is not necessary for us to hurt ourselves and one another in self-hating and self-defeating behaviors. We are free to be more of who we really are. We can be willing to wear our kente and our ankhs, our tie-dyes and wax prints, our cowrie shells and scarabs. We lay aside the restrictive garments of our enslavement, the corsets and bras of Europe. We are willing to allow our wide-bottomed beauty to be seen and felt beneath the shadows of our bubas. Our hair is freed to coil and curl as it will into the locks of ancient Egypt's patterning. We remember that our liberation begins with the renewal of our minds and that pressing and oppressing our hair "puts a ceiling on our brains."[15]

When our brains are free and our minds are clear, we remember to pour libation to our ancestors. We rekindle the knowing of ourselves as an ancient people. This is the knowledge we have to share with our sisters, young and old alike, in conversation and community, whether it is song-inspired or between friends. We acknowledge the ancestors, those whose names are no longer remembered, the ones who died in the anonymity of the middle passage and who are insistently demanding to be re-inspirited in us. We also recollect and gather up the living-dead ones whose names we do remember, who more recently walked the planet, whose images mirror our own looking out at us from photo albums and picture frames. These living-dead ones are now spirits still hovering among us. They are available to us, they can be spoken to and felt "in the rustling wind and moaning rocks." We are able to feel the presence of the yet-unborn ones, our future generations too. To these we also pour libation, welcoming them into our wombs and into our lives.

Mindful of our cultural roots and values, with both ancestors and future generations in tow, we are able to mediate culture to our community. We are agents of wisdom, moral choice, and meaning for African-Americans. By the rituals we create we are able to wrest order out of chaos. We take our indignation, our anger, and our alienation and turn it into salvation for our selves and those we love. In the face of insurmountable odds and the things that frighten us and shake our souls, we do not quiver. We replace fear with faith and live it out by refusing to be kept down. We let go of that which is not ours to handle, we surrender ourselves and our life's cares to God. This is our first line of defense in an inhospitable and dangerous world. We remember who we are and whose we are by keeping the lines of communication open to the creator by way of spirit. We are not afraid of spirit. We welcome its presence among us. When pressed to the wall of confusion and chaos witnessing a world over which we have precious little control, we do not despair. We stand up, we stand in the gap, we take a stand for ourselves in the circle of our ancient ones.

Notes

1. Maya Angelou, "Africa," in *Poems* (New York: Bantam Books, 1986) 77.

2. Nsenga Warfield-Coppock, *Afrocentric Theory and Applications*, vol. 1, *Adolescent Rites of Passage* (Washington, D.C.: Baobab Associates, Inc., 1990) 34.

3. Robert McClain, *Come Sunday: The Liturgy of Zion* (Nashville: Abingdon Press, 1990) 51.

4. A West African proverb quoted in Warfield-Coppock, *Afrocentric* 3.

5. From a conversation with Bernice Johnson Reagon.

6. Paul Lawrence Dunbar, "When Malindy Sings, in *The Complete Poems of Paul Laurence Dunbar* (New York: Dodd, Mead and Co., 1962) 132.

7. Zora Neale Hurston, *The Sanctified Church* (Berkeley, CA: Turtle Island, 1983) 91.

8. A West African proverb.

9. Carolyn M. Rodgers, "Shout" in *The Heart Is Ever Green* (Anchor Press, 1978) 33.

10. Charles Joyner, *Down by the Riverside: A South Carolina Slave Community* (Urbana: University of Chicago Press, 1984) 160.

11. Ysaye Marie Barnwell, *Singing in the African-American Tradition* (Homespun Tape Ltd., Box 694, Woodstock, NY) 8.

12. A West African proverb.

13. Albert J. Raboteau, *Slave Religion: The Invisible Institution of the Antebellum South* (New York: Oxford University Press, 1978) 35.

14. Douglas Baracsh, *New York Times* (1 November 1992) Section 2, p.27, column 1.

15. Alice Walker, "Oppressed Hair Puts a Ceiling on the Brain," in *Living by the Word: Selected Writings, 1973-1987* (San Diego: Harcourt, Brace, Jovanovich, 1988) 69.

13

Dismantling Patriarchy— A Redemptive Vision: Ritual and Feminist Critical Theology in Basic Ecclesial Communities

Anne R. Andersson

Thank you for the songs you sang in the midst of so much suffering, and thank you for the dancing. You affirm what I have known all along, that ritual is central to our soul's survival, that women are the celebrants of the mystery of life. The ability to find joy in the midst of sorrow and hope at the edge of despair is women's witness to courage and her gift of new life to all.[1]

PRISTINE CHRISTIANITY IS PRESENTLY EMPOWERING THE POOR AND oppressed in a new wave which began in Latin America through the charism of liberation theology. The movement is concretely expressed in the rise of small Basic Christian Ecclesial Communities that are emerging throughout the world and that are infusing a new breath of the Spirit into what had largely become a distorted Christianity—a Christianity allied with the wealthy elite classes.

The Basic Christian Community (BCC) movement, or in Spanish, *la comunidad de base*, or the Basic Ecclesial Community

(BEC) movement, *la comunidad eclesial de base*, is built upon outrage at the monumental injustices extant in the world—
hunger, poverty, exploitation, domination, oppression.
Though the outrage has caused a collective recognition of the
need to challenge the structures that are the predominant causes of oppression, the focus has, for the most part, had a male
face. Largely neglected in the response of the Christian communities has been the plight of women. Theologian Monika
Hellwig states that the human response of outrage in the face
of the violation of human rights rests on a sense of an "existential scream of pain or deprivation." "But," says Hellwig, "we
have to hear the scream first."[2] In general the cries of women
have been unheard and ignored largely because women's pain
has not been perceived by men to result from a violation of human rights. Thus causes have not been seriously addressed.
Sometimes it is the women themselves who have not understood their own inner turmoil. This paper examines the ritual
aspects of Basic Ecclesial Communities and the impact of feminist critical theology on the concept of base community, particularly as the concept is being translated to Roman Catholicism
in the United States.

What are Basic Ecclesial Communities? Their origins are
variously attributed, but their prototype is found in early
Christianity—in the various Christian communities and house
churches that emerged after the death and resurrection of Jesus. Monika Hellwig notes that these communities bring us
back to the beginnings of Christianity, including the "fervor of
those times." There is "an element of counterculture, an element of challenge, a fresh and vigorous appropriation of the
Gospel . . . a willingness to abandon private interests for the
common good and the common purpose."[3]

Basically these communities, as they have formed in Latin
America since the 1950s, are comprised of people at the base
or grassroots of society whose faith and praxis have been integrated through the joint efforts of lay people and pastoral
agents. The impetus for the emergence of these communities is
variously assigned to the religious and cultural factors that informed the Second Vatican Council. A pivotal point for the acceptance of the BEC movement as a positive force by the Roman Catholic hierarchical clerical structure was the Second
Council of Latin American Bishops, which convened in Medel-

lin, Columbia, in 1968. Also important was the Bishops' Conference at Puebla, Mexico, in 1979, which first recognized BEC ecclesiology. The addition of the word "ecclesial" to "Basic Christian Communities" signified a change in the bishops' understanding of these communities—Basic Ecclesial Communities, though recognized as "church," are theoretically under the auspices of the local Roman Catholic hierarchy, the priests and bishops, who are, in turn, under the authority of Rome.

Such communities have taken liberation theology as part of their identity with the Gospel of Jesus Christ, bringing it to bear directly on the practical aspects of the lives of the participants as they analyze their living conditions vis-a-vis the gospel message. The divine within these communities is envisaged as in the Exodus story, and Jesus is primarily the one who acts on behalf of the poor and marginalized. BECs, justice-oriented and embracing political action as praxis, always contain a worship dimension within which all participate—as the communitarian structure is intended to be egalitarian—and to which are brought problems, viewpoints, and tensions.

These problems, viewpoints, and tensions, which underpin both ritualizing and secular political action, have not been those of women. New perspectives in ritual tend to arise in a Christian community when the consciousness of women—not only the poor, but women as women—is raised regarding their situation, not only as the poor but specifically as women; ritualizing flows from awareness of lived condition. Christian Basic Ecclesial Communities could become for women, who comprise the majority of participants in Latin American communities, the spaces to share pain and joy, the sources of communal strength to bring anguish to action, the transformers of energy with which to begin radical remembering, the places to touch the Divine in a new way.

For example, since reality for poor women in Latin American countries includes so much violence and death,[4] secular political action might include daring deeds, and ritual action might involve remembering the brave actions. Remembering in El Salvador could, in itself, be considered a courageous act. Salvadorean Mothers of the Disappeared have kept alive the memory of members of their families who have disappeared, been murdered or who are political prisoners.[5] Often, activism has resulted in torture and death. One Salvadorean woman, a "human rights activist" who forced remembrance by exposing government violations, was burned and killed in 1983.[6] Through the radical interpretation/integration of the Gospel into their lives, "like Jesus of Nazareth, these women accept death as the price for 'refusing to abandon the radical activity of love—of expressing solidarity and reciprocity with the excluded ones'[7] in their midst." Remembering is courageous, "remembering is a holy act."[8]

Remembering is also life-support for women. Women-centered ritual introduces something new as it reaches/speaks to a sense and understanding of the divine that is not present in traditional ritual celebrations.[9] For example, women-centered rituals in Basic Ecclesial Communities that exist within a context of violence might center on the remembrance of the martyrdom of women with the understanding that the *locus* of divine presence at the time of the martyrdom was in the midst of the women's suffering. The focus of a ritual might be on rape, the particular form violence often takes in the lives of martyred women. In other communities rituals might concentrate on the healing power of Jesus in the form of solidarity and sisterhood in the face of incest, forced sterilization, abortion, hysterectomies, separation, divorce, emotional abuse.[10] More positively, women-centered rituals might celebrate a special day such as International Women's Day or in Portuguese, *Dia Internacional da Mulher*. On a more personal level, rituals might commemorate the natural life cycle, which would include the onset of menstruation or menopause.[11] Rosemary Ruether has outlined four sequences for women-centered rituals. These sequences, which transcend remembering, focus on four areas: the formation of the church as a community in liberation from patriarchy, on rites of healing from particular occasions of violence and crisis, on rites of the life cycle and on seasonal celebrations.[12]

Ritualizing by women in Latin American BECs is just beginning to happen. In actuality, secular political action has been the guiding reality. At present there are feminist base communities that create women-centered rituals, though these are usually not Basic Ecclesial Communities. Part of the reason for this lack might be the overall dearth of feminist consciousness within the majority of BECs. Another reason involves moves by the Roman Catholic hierarchy that signal suppression of feminist activism in Catholic Christian Communities. The role of women in these communities has changed both women and the concept of ministry in a way that is causing resistance and fear in hierarchical clerical circles. Although the *comunidades eclesiales de base* began and developed as a new way of being church in both the collegial structural format and the blending of theology and political action, Brazilian feminist theologian Ivone Gebara states that:

> the new element in this service [of women's ministries] is found in the way it responds to a certain number of the community's vital needs and in the fear that it is generating in those who are in charge of the churches and who are gradually losing their former prestige. Women's ministry is shaking up men's ministry, challenging their practice and the exercise of their authority.[13]

Sonia E. Alvarez, assistant professor of politics at the University of California, Santa Cruz, has another view. She analyzes the base community movement in Sao Paulo, Brazil, in relation to women as a negative force that keeps women in their place. She claims that the roles of women in these communities are too similar to the positions that women hold in their own families. Alvarez challenges that:

> liberation theology and the Christian-base community movement have made women more aware of themselves as *citizens* but not as *women*. When empowerment as citizens triggers women's consciousness of their gender-specific oppression, as occurred in two cases documented, the church has intervened to discourage this process of change.[14]

When raised consciousness in BECs causes the women to "question the powerful and masculine model of the internal structures of the church," the women are deemed "dangerous."[15]

Indeed, "dangerous" is an accurate descriptive term for the power latent in a base community, particularly when that community begins to understand itself as "in liberation from patriarchy."[16] The greatest "danger" is to the patriarchal order, as there is major transformative power within the Basic Ecclesial Community. Furthermore, I hold that recognition of this transformative power is at the root of the fear and resistance of those in clerical and other positions in the church.

New stirring in relation to feminist ritualizing is occurring within some base community and professional groups in areas of Bolivia and Brazil. When Maryknoll sister Lyn Kirkconnell describes her experience in the last three years within the Brazilian feminist movement and with groups of Christian women at the base and in academic circles, she indicates that the use of ritual has been "minimal."[17] However, very recently she has found that there has been a rising of interest in feminist spirituality within the Latin American women's movement in general[18] and a growing interest in feminist ritual by women in the BECs. Kirkconnell believes that the ground is fertile, with the future open for the development of feminist ritualizing, because women are responding to the sense of the divine in their own lives imaged in ways not previously available to them.[19] Women's ease with new modes in divine imaging and ritualizing is well summarized in the words of Elizabeth Johnson, who explains that "[w]omen realize that they participate in the image of the divine and so their own concrete reality can point toward this mystery."[20]

In response to the new interest within Brazil, Kirkconnell and her associate, Judy McDonnell, O.P., have developed a course on feminist spirituality that includes eighteen segments, each of which culminates in a ritual revolving around the theme of the course. The rituals, as Kirkconnell describes them:

> use all of our senses, including quiet reflective moments as well as sharing in groups, and have symbols from the faith backgrounds of the women (incense, candles, music, prayers, readings—scriptural and other offerings . . .). These symbols are used creatively, with all participating actively in the ritual. The themes deal with the course content and therefore represent a reclaiming of women's history and story.[21]

Kirkconnell believes that whenever the course has been offered "these rituals have played an important part in incarnating the [women's] journey."[22] As these two women have worked largely within limited sections of Bolivia and Brazil, their efforts are becoming known particularly in these areas. There have been various requests for their course. Several women's groups, including women in base communities, have contacted them and women among whom they work for input in creating women-centered rituals. Recently, Lutheran pastoral agents have also shown interest in their efforts.

In addition to the activity of the women of the BECs who are just beginning to create their own rituals, more has been happening regarding ritualizing in groups of professional religious leaders. In Chile, Peru, Argentina, and Brazil, and very likely in every other country in Latin America, small groups are forming of "mostly but not exclusively" professional religious women. These women are "pastors, church workers and [BEC] leaders who are frustrated with the limited horizons their churches offer for their emerging feminist spirituality." The groups "meet to share their evolving sense of the holy and to develop rituals that give expression to that presence." Radical remembering in these groups focuses on

> their own foremothers, the many forgotten women of history, including those women who have been martyred in Latin America in the past few decades as a result of their struggle for a more just society. They often sit in a circle, a 'holy space' and talk about how God is made manifest in their lives.[23]

Manifestation of divinity is at the heart of feminist theology, which in turn plays a key role in the formation of women-centered rituals. This paper focuses on three aspects of feminist theology: redemption, biblical hermeneutics, and Christology, with emphasis on the feminist theology of Rosemary Radford Ruether and Elisabeth Schüssler Fiorenza. It is important to understand that, as Ada Maria Isasi-Diaz explains, "the theological process is an intrinsic part of the liberation task because it is one of the ways in which the community becomes the agent of its own history."[24]

Central to the communities is the political confrontational stance. The importance of this stance lies in the tension created between the communities and the governmental or ecclesial institutions—for it is the same sort of tension which caused Jesus to be crucified and the early Christians to be persecuted, and which is the root of the persecution of activists within the BECs of today. The tension introduced by feminist theology arises from the confrontation of the imbalance in the power dynamics within the female-male relationship, an imbalance which, rooted in patriarchy, acts as the prototype for all forms of oppression and exploitation. This prototypical view has been the thesis of some feminist writing[25] and has also appeared in results of a 1944 study of racial problems in the United States by Swedish economist Gunnar Myrdal.[26]

It is in three dialectical relationships of the "household codes" of Aristotle's *Politics*, as these dialectics function within patriarchy, that feminist theology makes its most eloquent statement. Salvation, in a feminist theological perspective, rests in the balancing of the disproportionate nature of relationship found in the "codes"—the power relationships between three pairs, the master-slave, father-son, and husband-wife. The "codes" as they function in family, society, and church, are "concerned with the relationship between rulers and ruled in household and state."[27] In the understanding of Schüssler Fiorenza, the "codes" are better termed "patterns of patriarchal submission,"[28] as they are concerned with the "submissiveness and obedience of the socially weaker group—wives, slaves, children on the one hand and with the authority of the head of the household, the paterfamilias, on the other hand."[29] Schüssler Fiorenza further states that "liberation from patriarchal structures is not only explicitly articulated by Jesus but is in fact at the heart of the proclamation of the basileia of God."[30]

Rosemary Ruether is in agreement, as she states that "[i]n God's kingdom the corrupting principle of domination and subjugation will be overcome."[31] While Galatians 3:28 teaches that there are to be no such domination patterns in Christian communities, some early Christian communities, in order to escape persecution, adopted the patriarchal patterning of the codes as an outward show of allegiance to the state. Thus the codes are found in some New Testament texts and prophetically missing from others.

These household codes are important today. Political philosopher Susan Moller Okin contends that the "Aristotelian political ethics of the household code" is still operative in "contemporary American democratic society".[32] Societal structuring mirrors the patriarchal family—the paterfamilias in society takes the form of ruler, dictator, corporate CEO, or Roman pontiff. The Bible has been a significant political tool used by those in power to maintain the structure, particularly through a hermeneutic which likens the paterfamilias to God.

It is possible that the broad definition of patriarchy as father-ruled society or other definitions which place the domination problem solely in the hands of men are not sufficiently descriptive of the dynamics involved in dominating behavior, for women also oppress. The patriarchal order might be better clarified to mean any form of the oppressor-oppressed relationship. Redemption, in this context, would mean liberation for women and men from all forms of dominating behavior. Letty Russell states that "this wider meaning of patriarchy is descriptive of every form of exploitation . . . It refers to the way a society functions, not simply to particular actions of men in society."[33] She suggests that alternative modes in society be understood as "circles of interdependence."[34]

In light of the preceding feminist interpretation of salvation, the base community is a prime locus to begin the elimination of patriarchal patterning in all of its forms. This must take place not only within the community structure and its rituals, but must be incorporated into the inner organization of each family within each base community. It must also translate into confrontation with outside societal and ecclesial structures that support the patriarchal order. BECs are important, as they offer a promising new way of overcoming the repressive character of patriarchy as it is exhibited in the official Roman Church. Because the BECs remain intimately connected to the mainline Roman church and include clergy and religious who learn as they guide, the BECs are in the position of being able to transform a diseased ecclesial institutional structure. With change conceivable for church and society, the opportunity exists for the dismantling of patriarchy and with it the re-emergence of the vision of Jesus.

A second relevant aspect of feminist theology is feminist theological hermeneutics, which considers only those biblical texts that are free of patriarchal patterning to be revelatory. Feminist theological hermeneutics understands the gospel message and ministry of Jesus as liberating praxis and envisions Basic Ecclesial Communities as formed of people in liberation from patriarchy. Feminist theology applies a "critical evaluation and 'hermeneutics of suspicion' both to the content and the process of biblical interpretation as well as upon the texts themselves."[35] A "feminist hermeneutics of suspicion" goes beyond merely a "systematic analysis of androcentric texts [for it] understands these texts to be ideological articulations of men expressing, as well as maintaining, patriarchal historical conditions."[36] It is important to note that there was a plurality of early Christian communities, not all of which incorporated patriarchal patterning. The silent New Testament texts can be seen "as part of the submerged traditions of the egalitarian early Christian movement."[37] Schüssler Fiorenza notes that while only "remnants of the non-patriarchal early Christian ethos" are retrievable in the canon of the New Testament, they are visible enough to allow for an understanding that "women had the power and authority of the gospel, that they were central and leading individuals in the early Christian movement."[38]

The third aspect to be examined involves new thinking about Christian spiritual symbolism. One symbol being redefined by feminist theology is that of the Christ, with a significant new approach offered by Schüssler Fiorenza. Elizabeth Johnson has also provided valuable research in this same area in her new book, *She Who Is*. Schüssler Fiorenza has developed an argument which connects the female principle with Jesus. She accomplishes this through a reexamination of wisdom theology, part of the milieu of early Christianity, which understands the divine as sophia (wisdom), the feminine principle. She attempts to demonstrate that sophia theology radically linked sophia with Christ, while remaining also in communication with the goddess religions of the time, particularly with the worship of Isis. Such an early Christian community linkage of Jesus, sophia and the goddess religions has a three-fold positive consequence. A linkage of this magnitude would provide a possible means for Christians to incorporate qualities of goddess religions into Christianity and to acknowledge those aspects of Christianity that are of goddess religions. The connection would provide an avenue for Christian dialogue with these religions and would be a step toward solving the problem of the "maleness of Christ" polemic, which has been used to justify the exclusion of women from significant participation in Roman Catholic ecclesiology. In the understanding of the wisdom theology of early Christianity, "Sophia-Spirit, conceived as a semihypostatic divine female figure, was present in the worship service of the community. All received her spiritual gifts and powers."[39] "'The Spirit' was believed to be 'the Wisdom of God,' and the Spirit-Wisdom bestowed the gift of wisdom upon those who cultivated her gifts and who lived according to her calling."[40]

On the Jungian symbolic level, in Erich Neumann's description, the archetype of Sophia, who is actually the goddesses of antiquity, holds the attribute of spiritual transformation. In the process of spiritual transformation, the vessel is at the very center, for as Neumann states: "the symbolism of the vessel appears even at the highest level as the vessel of spiritual transformation."[41] Neumann further states that Sophia is "the feminine vessel, as vessel of rebirth and higher transformation"[42] and that:

> [a]lthough Christianity did its best to suppress it, this matriarchal symbolism has survived . . . not only in the cup of the Last Supper . . . The pre-Christian plunge bath signifies return to the mysterious uterus of the Great Mother and its water of life . . . [It] became in Christianity the baptismal bath of transformation.[43]

Neumann states that the Great Goddess archetype "Sophia . . . not only forms the earth and heaven of the retort that we call life, and is not only the whirling wheel revolving within it, but is also the supreme essence and distillation to which life in this world can be transformed."[44]

This concept of transformation matches the understanding of Teilhard de Chardin, whose cosmic vision of Christ also included the power of transformation. The cosmic Christ, understood within an evolving universe, permeates all of creation as a transformer, an evolver. Christ, the center, is the vessel of transformation—the same powerful understanding as in Roman Catholic liturgical celebration. Thus sophia and the cosmic Christ become intimately connected. I suggest that sophia and cosmic Christ are one.

If transformation were understood as the essence of the life of each base community, the evolution of the patriarchal order would be greatly advanced. Are there BECs specifically formed as transformative communities in liberation from patriarchy? An alternative movement that emerged in the United States in 1983 is presently spreading globally. Known as the Women-Church movement, a term originated by Schüssler Fiorenza, its focus is the feminist theology of friendship/reconciliation. Because of this focus on friendship as guiding metaphor, Women-Church holds great promise for the future. As described by Ruether, "Women-Church means neither leaving the church as a sectarian group, nor continuing to fit into it on its terms. It means establishing bases for a feminist critical culture and celebrational community that have some autonomy."[45] Although not separatist, there is the understanding that some initial separatism must take place in order for women to be able, in a non-hostile environment, to create Gospel and liturgy from their own experiences, to reclaim biblical stories through feminist hermeneutics, to be in touch with the Divine Feminine. Because both Ruether and Schüssler Fiorenza conclude that the Jesus movement occurred within Judaism as an attempt to reform it, this understanding provides support for the present maintenance of a connection to the official religion by the Women-Church movement. Although the connection is ultimately desirable, feminist groups have not only chosen to separate but have also not been welcomed by the Roman hierarchy. Like other base communities that practice a critical hermeneutics of suspicion, which includes criticism of the Roman hierarchical church, feminist communities have been suppressed and forced out of communion with their local dioceses.[46]

Women-Church, though certainly not solely Roman Catholic, began largely as a Roman Catholic movement. It emerged in the United States from the frustration generated in those women who sought ordination in the institutional church as their efforts were blocked and as fruitful dialogue with the hierarchy became unavailable.[47] Focus for change shifted from seeking ordination to being church.[48] Informed by the tenets of the Second Vatican Council, nurtured by feminist theology, and fueled by outrage at ecclesial oppression within the Roman Catholic Church, Women-Church also drew inspiration from the comunidades de base. Similarities to the BECs lie in the fact that Women-Church groups are small and local, have a worship dimension, and are a way of living faith.[49] On another level, groups could be considered "base" or "of the poor" even when comprised of women of the middle and upper economic strata of society. Mary Hunt states that "poor also refers, in a more generic way, to those who have been marginalized by society."[50] Roger Garaudy has described the base as "that part of society's population simultaneously deprived of possessing, power, and knowledge. What characterizes the base," states Garaudy, "is the fact that it has been robbed of a future that belongs to it, that the power 'at the top' does not permit it to create its own history . . ."[51] Thus, in a global sense, all women are oppressed, all women are of the base.

The Women-Church groups are interconnected through large national conferences held periodically, at which more than twenty different countries have been represented. In addition to the small groups, Women-Church Convergence, a coalition of forty communities, also as a connective agent. The focus in Women-Church communities, each of which remains autonomous, is on "reflection, celebration and action on the understanding of redemption as liberation from patriarchy."[52] Some of the groups are liturgical, some, "on college campuses, are short-term," some include men, some welcome children. For some people they provide "the only worship experience," for others they supplement local parish church attendance.[53] Aspects of the communal experience include study, liturgy, social praxis and collective life.[54]

Rosemary Ruether understands that "probably the most dramatic expression of new liturgical comunities in the United States is the development of feminist liturgies."[55] Rituals in feminist liturgical communities "are written and shaped to express the root message of redemption as liberation from sexism." Liturgical rite "opens up the deeper dimension of transformed life that refers us back to ordinary life with renewed energies and consciousness."[56] The enlightened vision that understands redemption as liberation from patriarchy can be achieved by taking the risk of associating with radical feminism. One encounter with Mary Daly's book, *Gyn/ecology*, is enough to bring about the type of conversion that is a "leap to a new consciousness that renounces the ideologies that sought to justify the systems of oppression and seeks an alternative world where truth and good relationships prevail . . ."[57]

Women-Church promises to be a positive force for liberation from patriarchy and all forms of oppression—if it maintains its initial fervor and honesty and if it does not degenerate into a myopic political organization bent on self-preservation, as so often happens when a movement matures. In order for Women-Church, as a movement, to be fully successful, it must maintain communication with diverse feminist theologies, for example "mujerista theology, a Hispanic women's liberation theology."[58]

Also important, because of its close ties to the basic female-male imbalance, is womanist theology, a term defined by Alice Walker referring to black women's liberation theology. One of its important insights is that an understanding of racial issues has preceded and informed the feminist struggles of both the nineteenth and twentieth centuries. Pauli Murray states that "although tremendous differences existed between white women and black slaves in actual status and in their relations with the dominant class, the paternalistic idea placed the slave[59] 'beside women and children in the power of the pater-familias'."[60] As women of all colors suffer under the "paternalistic idea," perspectives must be linked, each to inform the other, not only to unite women in their struggle against patriarchy, but also to expand understanding of the variant forms that patriarchal patterning takes in the lives of culturally diverse women.

While differences are important to acknowledge on one level as women's needs vary so greatly, it is still crucial for feminist theologians to keep sight of overall patriarchal patterning, so that women will be enabled to clearly see how patriarchy is operative in the lives of all women. Mary Hunt states that "this dynamic is something which many adherents of women-church have internalized . . . We have seen that each form of oppression is interconnected with other forms . . ."[61] A good example of this global consciousness-raising is found in Daly's *Gyn/ecology*. In outlining the specific forms of patriarchal mutilation and murder of women in China, India, Africa, Europe, and the United States, Daly remains open to the diverse situations of women. In linking these as part of an overall pattern, she is able to keep the pattern visible and is also able to support her global statement that "patriarchy is itself the prevailing religion of the entire planet."[62]

Similarity within dissimilarity must remain in tension to keep the general patriarchal pattern visible. Women must see women as sisters, as friends of the women-church movement. When sisterhood of this sort happens on a massive and global scale, the foundations of the patriarchal order will be shaken. Only when global outrage turns to outcry, leads to inner transformation, and inspires outside action will the possibility exist for collapse of the old order.

To summarize, the *comunidades eclesiales de base*, based in Latin America and currently in a global translation, are a new way of being church that allows an intimate connection to the institutional churches of the various Christian denominations of which they are a part. Ritualizing within the communities has generally not been emphasized, though there is a growing interest in feminist spirituality and women-centered rituals. The dimension of feminist theology is creating an impact on new communities in the United States and elsewhere, in the form of the women-church movement. In Latin America, Women-Church—or, in Spanish, *Mujer-Iglesia*—communities currently exist (for example, in Chile and Argentina[63]), and there is confidence that there will be an increase in such groups in the future, as the budding interest in feminist spirituality continues to develop. Feminist theology completes the "hermeneutic circle" of Juan Luis Segundo:[64] women who have undergone the process of conscientization (or consciousness-raising), become "self-identified."[65] They experience a tension between self-understanding and the position of women in society and in church which leads to scrutiny of prevailing androcentric theological systems. A new insight that theology was formulated by men in the interest of patriarchal male structures leads women to question prevailing androcentric interpretations of Scripture. A feminist perspective results in a new interpretation of Scripture that takes into account both androcentric language and the patriarchal tendencies of biblical writers.

In conclusion, a quote from Ruether's book, *Women-Church*, seems appropriate: the new community of Women-Church, which is rapidly becoming a global movement, envisions a form of feminism which "is able to constantly build an integral vision of a new humanizing culture beyond patriarchy without becoming closed or sectarian toward any living cultural option or human community. It remains open to authentic spirit wherever it is found and it extends to all the invitation to join a new dance of life without which life itself may not survive."[66]

What could be more hopeful for the future than harmony in a ritual dance of the human in female-male form?

Notes

1. Miriam Therese Winter, *WomanPrayer WomanSong: Resources for Ritual* (Illinois: Meyer Stone Books, 1987) 5.
2. Monika Hellwig, "The Quest for Common Ground in Human Rights—A Catholic Reflection," in *Human Rights in the Americas: The*

Struggle for Consensus, ed. Alfred Hennelly, S.J. and John Langan, S.J. (Washington, D.C.: Georgetown University Press, 1982) 160.

3. Monika Hellwig, foreword to the English Edition of Marcello de Azevedo, *Basic Ecclesial Communities in Brazil: The Challenge of a New Way of Being Church,* trans. John Drury (Washington, D.C.: Georgetown University Press, 1987) xi.

4. Jane M. Grovijahn, "Grabbing Life Away From Death: Women and Martyrdom in El Salvador," *Journal of Feminist Studies in Religion* 7:2 (Fall 1991): 21-27.

5. Ibid. 23; Maria Pilar Aquino, "Women's Participation: A Catholic Perspective," in *With Passion and Compassion: Third World Women Doing Theology,* ed. Virginia Fabella, M.M. and Mercy Amba Oduyoye (Maryknoll, NY: Orbis Books, 1989) 163.

6. Grovijahn, "Women and Martyrdom in El Salvador" 23-24.

7. Beverly Wildung Harrison, *Making the Connections: Essays in Feminist Social Ethics* (Boston: Beacon Press, 1985) 18, quoted in Grovijahn, "Women and Martyrdom in El Salvador" 28.

8. Grovijahn, "Women and Martyrdom in El Salvador" 24.

9. Telephone conversation with Lyn Kirkconnell, M.M., March, 1993.

10. Lyn Kirkconnell, M.M and Judy McDonnell, O.P., unpublished pamphlet, "O ritual para As Mulheres" (Sao Paulo, Brazil, n.d.) 4; Rosemary Radford Ruether, *Women-Church: Theology and Practice of Feminist Liturgical Communities* (San Francisco: Harper & Row, 1986) 151-168.

11. Kirkconnell and McDonnell, "O Ritual" 3; Ruether, *Women-Church* 188-190, 204-206.

12. Ruether, *Women-Church* 107-121, Chapters 7-10.

13. Ivone Gebara, "Women Doing Theology in Latin America," in Fabella, ed., *With Passion and Compassion* 133.

14. Sonia E. Alvarez, "Women's Participation in the Brazilian 'People's Church: A Critical Appraisal," *Feminist Studies* 16:2 (Summer 1990): 382.

15. Aquino, "Women's Participation: Catholic," in Fabella, ed., *With Passion and Compassion* 162-163.

16. Rosemary Radford Ruether, *Sexism and God-Talk: Toward a Feminist Theology* (Boston: Beacon Press, 1983) 205; and *Women-Church* 5-6.

17. Lyn Kirkconnell, letter and telephone conversation, March, 1993.

18. Kirkconnell, telephone conversation, March, 1993; Mary Judith Ress, "Latin American Feminists Finding Their Voice," *National Catholic Reporter* (13 September 1991): 7-8.

19. Kirkconnell, telephone conversation, March, 1993.

20. Elizabeth A. Johnson, *She Who Is: The Mystery of God in Feminist Theological Discourse* (New York: Crossroad, 1992) 46.

21. Kirkconnell, letter, March, 1993.

22. Ibid.

23. Ress, "Latin American Feminists" 7.

24. Ada Maria Isasi-Diaz and Yolanda Tarango, *Hispanic Women: Prophetic Voice in the Church* (San Francisco: Harper and Row, 1988) 6.

25. See Gerda Lerner, *The Creation of Patriarchy* (New York: Oxford University Press, 1986).

26. Gunnar Myrdal, *An American Dilemma* (New York: Harper & Bros., 1944) Appendix 5, "A Parallel to the Negro Problem" 1073-1078; quoted in Gayraud S. Wilmore and James H. Cone, eds., *Black Theology: A Documentary History, 1966-1979* (Maryknoll, NY: Orbis Books, 1979) 402, n.18.

27. Ibid. 73.

28. Ibid.

29. Ibid. 71.

30. Elisabeth Schüssler Fiorenza, *In Memory of Her: A Feminist Theological Reconstruction of Christian Origins* (New York: Crossroad, 1983) 151.

31. Ruether, *Sexism and God-Talk* 30.

32. Susan Moller Okin, *Women in Western Political Thought* (Princeton, NJ: Princeton University Press, 1979) 276, quoted in Elisabeth Schüssler Fiorenza, *Bread Not Stone: The Challenge of Feminist Biblical Interpretation* (Boston: Beacon Press, 1984) 89, n. 53.

33. Letty Russell, "Partnership in Models of Renewed Community," *The Ecumenical Review* 40 (January 1988): 17.

34. Ibid.

35. Schüssler Fiorenza, *Bread Not Stone* 139.

36. Schüssler Fiorenza, *Memory* 60.

37. Schüssler Fiorenza, *Bread Not Stone* 112.

38. Schüssler Fiorenza, *Memory* 35-36.

39. Ibid. 220.

40. B.A. Pearson, *The Pneumatikos-Psychikos Terminology in 1 Corinthians* (SBL Diss. 12; Missoula, MT: Scholars Press, 1973); quoted in Schüssler Fiorenza, *Memory* 219-220.

41. Erich Neumann, *The Great Mother: An Analysis of the Archetype*, Bollingen Series XLVII, trans. Ralph Manheim (New Jersey: Princeton University Press, 1955) 326.

42. Ibid. 329.

43. Ibid. 326.

44. Ibid. 325.

45. Ruether, *Women-Church* 62.

46. For further study on the separatism phenomenon, see discussion of Basic Christian Communities in Italy in Ruether, *Women-Church* 30-31; also Ed Grace, "Basic Christian Communities—Italy," *Christianity and Crisis* 41:14 (21 September 1981): 236; forced separatism has been the experience of Christian Women: Quo Vadis?, a group which this author co-founded in Weston, Connecticut in 1983. An unrealized goal of the association has been to work in communion with the local Diocese of Bridgeport on behalf of women in the diocese.

47. Mary E. Hunt, "Women-Church in a Global Perspective," an article originally delivered as a lecture at a workshop, "An Experience of Women-Church," held at The Tiltenberg, a conference center run by the Grail, outside of Amsterdam, The Netherlands, December 1987, 6.

48. Ibid. 9.

49. Lyn Kirkconnell, telephone conversation, March, 1993.

50. Mary E. Hunt, "Social Justice Expressions of Women-Church," an article originally delivered as a lecture at the workshop "An Experience of Women-Church," The Grail, 2.

51. Roger Garaudy, "A base no marxismo e no cristianismo," *Concilium* 104/4 (1975): 434-436, quoted in Marcello de Carvalho Azevedo, S.J., *Basic Ecclesial Communities in Brazil* 75.

52. Ruether, *Sexism and God-Talk* 205.

53. Mary E. Hunt, "Women-Church in a Global Perspective" 14-15.

54. Ruether, *Women-Church* 91-93.

55. Ibid. 31.

56. Ruether, *Sexism and God-Talk* 210-211.

57. Ruether, *Women-Church* 126.

58. Ada Maria Isasi-Diaz, "Viva La Diferencia!" in "Special Section on Appropriation and Reciprocity in Womanist/Mujerista/Feminist Work," *Journal of Feminist Studies in Religion* 8:2 (Fall 1992): 98-102.

59. Pauli Murray, "Black Theology and Feminist Theology: A Comparative View," in Wilmore and Cone, *Black Theology* 402.

60. Gunnar Myrdal, *American Dilemma* 1073; quoted in Pauli Murray, "Black Theology and Feminist Theology," in Wilmore and Cone, *Black Theology* 402.

61. Mary E. Hunt, "Social Justice Expressions of Women-Church" 3-4.

62. Mary Daly, *Gyn/ecology* (Boston: Beacon Press, 1978) 39.

63. Letter from Mary E. Hunt, Co-director Women's Alliance for Theology, Ethics and Ritual, Silver Spring, Maryland, January 29, 1990.

64. Juan Luis Segundo, *The Liberation of Theology*, trans. John Drury (Maryknoll, NY: Orbis Books, 1976) 7-38; Alfred Hennelly, S.J., *Theology for a Liberating Church: The New Praxis of Freedom* (Washington, D.C.: Georgetown University Press, 1989) 39-41.

65. Schüssler Fiorenza, *Bread Not Stone* xv.

66. Ibid. 40.

Contributors

Anne R. Andersson teaches in the theology department of St. John's University, Jamaica, New York. She is a co-founder of Christian Women: Quo Vadis?, a Connecticut-based feminist Christian community which, in addition to consciousness-raising and education, creates women-centered rituals.

Sheila Webster Boneham earned her Ph.D. in folklore at Indiana University, where she initiated a course on women and folklore. She has taught at Indiana University, the University of Maryland, Kuwait University, and the University of Tunis.

Barbara Borts, currently rabbi of Temple Beth-El, Geneva, New York, trained for the rabbinate in London, England. She has worked in synagogues in London, lectured and written on Jewish women and social issues, and founded the Social Issues Group of the Reform Synagogues of Great Britain.

Linda Coleman is associate professor of English at the University of Maryland. She has her Ph.D. in linguistics from the University of California, Berkeley. Her research has focused on the language of religion and the language of advertising.

Melva Wilson Costen is Helmar E. Nielsen Professor of Worship and Music at the Interdenominational Theological Center, Atlanta, Georgia. She is an Elder in the Presbyterian Church (U.S.A.), serves as Moderator of the denomination's Theology and Worship Ministry Unit, and was a member of the committee that compiled the 1990 hymnal, *Hymns, Psalms and Spiritual Songs*.

Dana Everts-Boehm received her Ph.D. in folklore from Indiana University. She is currently a folklife specialist with the Missouri Folk Arts Program at the Museum of Art and Archeology, University of Missouri-Columbia.

Karen Sue Hybertsen, an ordained minister in the Presbyterian Church (U.S.A.), received her Ph.D. from Drew University. She has taught at County College of Morris (New Jersey) and Drew Seminary.

Amitiyah Elayne Hyman is parish associate at the New York Avenue Presbyterian Church in Washington, D.C. She was formerly chaplain for the All African Ministries at American University in Washington, D.C. and an instructor at Montgomery Community College, Takoma Park, Maryland.

Diann L. Neu is co-founder and co-director of WATER, the Women's Alliance for Theology, Ethics and Ritual, in Silver Spring, Maryland. An author and co-author of many publications, she has designed many rituals for national and international conferences, as well as for her own women-church base community in the Washington, D.C. area.

Lesley A. Northup, assistant professor of Religion and Culture at Florida International University, received her Ph.D. in historical theology from The Catholic University of America in Washington, D.C. Her area of specialization is ritual studies. Her book, *The 1892 Book of Common Prayer,* will be published later this year.

Kathryn Allen Rabuzzi teaches in the Department of English and Textual Studies at Syracuse University. A founding editor of the journal *Literature and Medicine,* she is the author of *The Sacred and the Feminine: Towards a Theology of Housework* and of *MOtherself: A Mythic Analysis of Motherhood.*

Carole A. Rayburn is a clinical, consulting, and research psychologist with research in the areas of stress in clergy and women and spirituality. Dr. Rayburn is a fellow of The American Psychological Association and is regional chair for the APA's division on religious issues.

Sandy Eisenberg Sasso was the first woman ordained rabbi from the Reconstructionist Rabbinical College and the first to serve a Conservative congregation. The author of various articles on women and religion and of a much-praised children's book, *God's Paintbrush*, she is currently rabbi of Congregation Beth-El-Zedeck in Indianapolis, Indiana.

Shermie Shafer is an ordained Unitarian Universalist minister whose experience includes congregational ministry, hospital chaplaincy, pastoral psychotherapy, and marriage and family therapy. She currently lives and works in Indianapolis, Indiana, where she is involved in varied ecumenical endeavors.